The RIM TO RIM Road

Will Hamblen and the Crossing of Texas' Palo Duro Canyon

E. Hamblen

With a new introduction by Vicki Hamblen

Lubbock · Texas Plains Trail Books

*The Rim to Rim Road: Will Hamblen and
the Crossing of Texas' Palo Duro Canyon*
by E. Hamblen
New edition, with introduction by Vicki Hamblen

Texas Plains Trail Books
Texas Plains Trail Region
P. O. Box 88, Lubbock, Texas 79408-0088 USA
www.TexasPlainsTrail.com/books

Rim to Rim copyright © 1971 by E. Hamblen
Originally published by Nortex Offset Publications, Inc.
Quanah and Wichita Falls, Texas
New portions of this edition copyright © 2014 by Stewart Hamblen
and Carol Hamblen Kilchriste

All rights reserved. No part of this book may be reproduced in any form or by any electronic or mechanical means, including information storage and retrieval systems, without written permission from the publisher or author, except in the case of a reviewer, who may quote brief passages embodied in a critical article or in a review.

Manufactured in the United States of America

10 9 8 7 6 5 4 3 2 1

ISBN 978-0-9906429-0-9 (trade paperback)

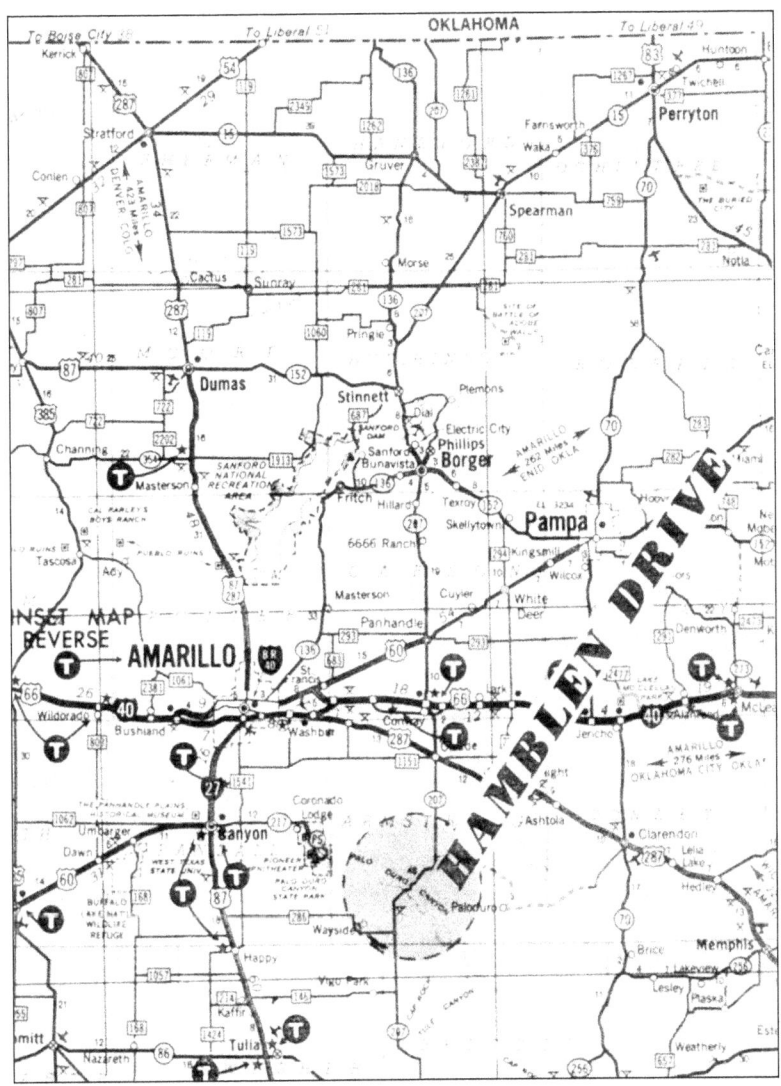

Map of Texas Panhandle, circa 1971, showing location of Hamblen Drive across Palo Duro Canyon in Armstrong County

William Henry Hamblen, drawing by Lynn Canafax

Contents

List of Illustrations 6
Hamblen Family Tree 8
Eutha Hamblen's *Rim to Rim*:
   A Historical Introduction 9
Dedication 15
Foreword 17
Chapter 1 19
Chapter 2 27
Chapter 3 31
Chapter 4 35
Chapter 5 41
Chapter 6 46
Chapter 7 53
Chapter 8 55
Chapter 9 59
Chapter 10 62
Chapter 11 64
Chapter 12 69
Chapter 13 71
Chapter 14 73
Chapter 15 75
Chapter 16 79
Chapter 17 82
Chapter 18 87
Chapter 19 89
Chapter 20 92
Chapter 21 94
Chapter 22 97
Chapter 23 101
Chapter 24 105
Chapter 25 108
Chapter 26 110
Acknowledgments 113
For Further Reading 113
About the Texas Plains Trail Region 114
Index 115

List of Illustrations

Most of the drawings that were untitled in the original edition appear without captions in the new edition.

Map of Texas Panhandle, circa 1971 3
Drawing of William Henry Hamblen 4
Eutha Mae Strawn Hamblen 9
Drawing of two women and boy on farm 20
Drawing of boy ploying behind mule 22
Cynthia Ann Parker and Prairie Flower 30
Quanah Parker 30
Drawing of rider on bucking horse 33
Drawing of house and windmill on prairie 38
Cowboys and visitors at C. T. Ward chuck wagon 50
Chuck wagon and tent used on ranches 50
R. M. Irick's freighters moving house from
 Dimmitt to Plainview 50
Will Hamblen on horseback 52
Drawing of young Will Hamblen 54
Will and Ada Hamblen wedding-day portrait, 1900 57
Will and Ada Hamblen with children Nellie and
 Alfred in their laps 58
"Canyon Road to Link South and North Plains,"
 Fort Worth Star-Telegram, March 11, 1937 75
Hamblen Drive, the "Rim to Rim Road," 2012 76
Drawing of horse-drawn wagon and driver 77
W. H. [Will] Hamblen campaign card 80
Drawing of draft team on Rolling Plains 83
Mule team on Rolling Plains 83
Hamblen family home, Wayside, Armstrong County,
 circa 1940s 84
W. H. (Will) Hamblen and family, circa 1934 84
Dust storm during the 1930s 90
Drawing of Wayside church and school building 94
Wayside Community Church, circa 1971 95
Drawing of dugout house 101

S. P. Hamblen Family historical marker, 2012 102
Hamblen Drive, early photos 104
Hamblen Drive, aerial photo 106
Hamblen Drive, showing bridge across Prairie Dog
    Town Fork of the Red River, 1968 106
Will Hamblen 110
Will Hamblen, late in life, driving mule team 111
Hamblen Drive historical marker, 2013 112

Hamblen Family Tree

- Sterling Phillip Hamblen & Margaret Jane McGee
  - William Henry Harrison "Will" Hamblen & Ada Sprayberry
    - Alfred Sterling Hamblen & Eutha Mae Strawn
      - Harvey Ray Hamblen
      - Alfred Beryl Hamblen
      - Carol Hamblen
      - Willliam Henry "Sonny" Hamblen
      - Stewart Warner "Guy" Hamblen
    - Nellie Evellyn Hamblen & Ira Hobson Burrow
    - Doris Lucille Hamblen & Travis Arrington Gillham
    - Ida Mae Hamblen & Carl Foster Rogers
    - Viola Hamblen & John Henry Perceval "Harry" Ward
    - Osce Lou Hamblen & E. J. "Jack" Parsons
    - Henry Tipton Hamblen & Flora Bernice Harris
    - Ramona Hamblen & James Carlton Fulton
    - Oleff McElroy Hamblen
  - William Alfred Sprayberry & Elizabeth Tipton

The descendants of Will and Ada's nine adult children are numerous; only Alfred's progeny (the generation appearing in this book) are shown here.

Eutha Hamblen's *Rim to Rim*: A Historical Introduction

MOST OF THE HISTORY AND POPULAR LORE of the Texas Panhandle seems to focus on Charles Goodnight and the famous JA Ranch of the late nineteenth century. But the book titled *Rim to Rim,* first published in 1971, concerns a lesser known but also fascinating history of the settling of a community and a man who was a trail blazer. It's a story of one man's persistence in pursuing his dream for a road that would connect a county, boost trade, and make daily life on the frontier a bit easier.

More than a century after Will Hamblen started imagining a road that would traverse America's second largest canyon, there are people every day who travel across Palo Duro Canyon from Claude, Texas, and don't know they're traveling Hamblen Drive. The paved, two-lane state road offers a beautiful view of curves, valleys, flat plains, and red clay walls. Many consider it one of the most scenic drives in the Lone Star State.

Eutha Mae Strawn Hamblen

Much has changed since the publication of *Rim to Rim* in 1971. Palo Duro Canyon State Park has become one of the nation's favorite park destinations, and the musical drama *Texas,* first performed in 1965, has become one of its most beloved outdoor dramas. The population of Armstrong County has grown to more than 1,900, though Will's community of Wayside has dwindled to only a few families. Texas Highway 207 has been widened and repaved. *Rim to Rim* went into a second printing, but soon sold out and became a collector's item. Through it all, Will Hamblen's family has learned new information and obtained additional photographs.

The book's author, Eutha Mae Strawn Hamblen (1902–1984), was a wife, a mother of six children, a homemaker, an educator, a student, and a volunteer. She also worked outside the home in her later years. She taught at Wayside School, where she met Alfred Sterling Hamblen, the first child of Will and Ada Hamblen to survive to adulthood. Eutha and Alfred married in May 1925.

Eutha was intelligent, a hard worker and a strong woman. After most of her children were grown, she attended classes at Amarillo College. She worked for an insurance company in Canyon, Texas, then in the registrar's office at West Texas State University (now West Texas A&M University). Eutha was a bookkeeper and tax preparer for various clients.

After she retired, Eutha volunteered with the Panhandle-Plains Historical Museum and the Canyon Senior Citizens. In the spring and fall of 1969 she took creative writing classes at West Texas State University, where her instructor, Kathleen Collins, encouraged her to write a book. *Rim to Rim* was privately published by Nortex Offset Publications of Quanah and Wichita Falls, Texas, in a hardcover edition of 112 pages, bound in red cloth with gold foil stamping on the cover and spine, and featured illustrations by Eutha's friends and classmates (many of whose names are lost to us now) as well as family and historical photographs. (The first printing can be identified by its regrettable misspelling "Hamblem" on the spine, an error corrected in the second printing.) The Panhandle-Plains Historical Museum held a book signing on January 16, 1972.

Most of the earliest wagon and automobile routes in Texas followed earlier Indian trails. Though American citizens had been clamoring for better roads since the 1910s, and Texas saw the development of the first all-weather transcontinental routes, such as the Bankhead Highway, starting around 1915, roads in the Panhandle as late as the 1920s were low-grade and unpaved. Public road improvements were done by men whose land bordered the road. During the Great Depression the Public Works Administration Act enabled citizens to be paid for their work—a dollar a day, to the men who worked on Hamblen Drive.

William Henry Harrison Hamblen (1876–1952) dreamed of a road across Palo Duro Canyon. Will wanted the residents of Wayside, on the south side of the twenty-mile-wide canyon, to be able to conduct county business in Claude, on the north side. Residents of the southern part of Armstrong County had to travel 120 miles around via the cities of Canyon and Amarillo to reach their county seat to vote, serve on juries, and handle other vital matters. Even riding a horse across the canyon was steep, dangerous, and slow.

In 1905 Will made a crude road following buffalo trails. The road started east of the Community Church in Wayside, then snaked down into the canyon for six miles. Will enlisted help of neighbors to cut the trail. Eventually this road became impassable without continuous maintenance.

Will decided to run for Armstrong County commissioner in 1928, hoping to provide citizens south of the canyon with representation and to acquire funds for improving his road. He won the election and received assistance. Will would be away from home two to three days at a stretch in order to attend county commissioners' meetings. In 1933, the road became passable from Wayside to Claude by automobiles, significantly reducing the time that Will spent attending commission meetings. Will and local workers were able to put in culverts and drain ditches.

In 1937, the State of Texas and the Federal Bureau of Public Roads at last cooperated to draft an adequate road-building program. Will and Armstrong County Judge Henry E. Herndon were instrumental in connecting the South Plains and the North Plains through Palo Duro Canyon. Will's road received further improvements with Works Progress Administration (WPA) funds. With these updates, the road was re-engineered to connect Claude to Silverton, bypassing Wayside.

November 1954 brought the welcome news that Hamblen Drive would be paved from Wayside to the Prairie Dog Town Fork of the Red River and would connect with the farm-to-market road south of Claude, and a bridge would be constructed across the river. The highway from Claude to Silverton became part of Texas Highway 207.

Rim to Rim is the personal and dramatic story of Anglo pioneers who settled a new land and one's man dream for a road to cross it. The settlers of Will Hamblen's day were hard-working men and women who wanted a better life for themselves and their families. Eutha Hamblen's record of the hardships they faced, and the particular details of their lives, help preserve the larger scope of Texas history.

Eutha told the story as she'd learned it from her ancestors and neighbors, and her telling is a product of their outlook, and their times. Historians know much more, now, about people such as Comanche chief Quanah Parker and his mother, Cynthia Ann Parker, comanchero trader José Tafoya, and General Ranald S. Mackenzie. We strive to speak of such historical figures with greater sensitivity to their lives and their cultures. But we cannot replace, or recast, the facts or experiences of history that only Eutha's work has contributed to the written record. We can only take what she has left us, and reexamine it in the light of evolving understanding.

Eutha's distinctive voice has been left unaltered here. Only obvious typographical errors and misspellings have been changed, along with purely mechanical features of punctuation, capitalization, and the like, to conform with standard practice. Where I am aware of factual errors in Eutha's account, I have noted so. This new edition adds numerous photographs, while keeping (and sometimes reordering) all of the original ones, and also adding an index, a valuable aid to researchers.

I first read *Rim to Rim* after my family received the book at my grandmother's signing party. I had learned a few months earlier, at the dedication of a Texas state historical marker in 1970, that my great-grandfather had built a road. My family aren't the kind of people who toot their own horn. To me, this book was worth telling others about—future generations needed to know about Hamblen Drive. I've since read the book many times, and every time I come away learning something new that I missed the time before.

History is an exciting subject for me; it always has been and I guess always will be. It's exciting to me that history happened right in my own back yard.

Vicki Hamblen
July 2014

Dedicated to the memory of
my father-in-law, Will Hamblen,
and the many pioneers who paved
a better road for us to follow

FOREWORD BY E. HAMBLEN

WILLIAM HENRY HAMBLEN WAS A MAN WITH A DREAM.

He was a pioneer with a purpose, a trail blazer, a man of action and persistence. He left a monument to his dream: State Highway 207, also known simply as Hamblen Drive.

Wes Izzard, editor of the *Amarillo Daily News,* paid tribute to Will and his persistent efforts at building his road.

When the road was dedicated, Mr. Izzard wrote:

The new highway across the Palo Duro Canyon is a monument to a quiet, persistent farmer named W. H. Hamblen. It was forty years ago that Farmer Hamblen first started work on the trail across the canyon. We can think of no better memorial to him than markers on both sides of the canyon, proclaiming the highway as Hamblen Drive.

Laura V. Hamner, historian and writer, spent many years researching the pioneer settlers in the Panhandle. She paid tribute to them over the air in her weekly radio broadcast and in her newspaper column. She spent three Sunday mornings on Will Hamblen. In her newspaper column, she wrote:

Will built a road across the Palo Duro Canyon to help his friends in making the dangerous crossing. That's what I would like to do. I'd like to build a road. I'd like to smooth the path for others. He was one of the greatest men that I have ever known. He was just a farmer like others in his community, and yet he was so big of soul that he could not live for himself alone. He thought of others and planned for the future of others. He worked long, hard hours alone that others might benefit from his labors. He dreamed and worked to give form to his dream. He was a great man, and yet the pages of history will not bear record of his name for he was "just a farmer." Who of those who drive across the beautiful Palo Duro Canyon road below Claude will know that they are traveling a trail that was the great objective in the life of one man, Will Hamblen of Wayside?

Following her series of Sunday morning broadcasts on the life of Will, Miss Hamner received this protest. "Why do you spend so much time on Will Hamblen? He was just a farmer."

The above quotation was her answer to this criticism. What makes a man just a —? A hard-working man? An honest man whose word was as sure as his written signature? A religious man? A man of integrity? Will was all of these, but Will was, also, a man with a dream.

207 TEXAS

Chapter 1

Sterling Philip Hamblen was fourteen years old when the Civil War created the Mason-Dixon Line. He was too young to join the Confederate Army, so he cleaned and loaded the guns for those who had [joined].

He married Jane McGee and moved to Mulberry, Tennessee. To this union were born three children. The older children were Mattie and Fannie. A boy, William Henry, was born on March 12, 1876. When Will was one year old, his mother died. Mattie and Fannie became housekeepers for their father and nursemaids for their brother.

The Ku Klux Klan became active in 1878. Along with many other families, he [Sterling Hamblen] left Tennessee for Texas. The families formed a wagon train. Some of the wagons were drawn by oxen, others by horses and mules. The cattle were driven by the men and children walking along the trail. The cows were milked each day, providing food for the children.

Although Will was only about two years old, crossing the great Mississippi River left a lasting impression. The river had not been dredged and narrowed by dikes and levees. It was a broad expanse of shallow water. The ferry was poled across since it was too wide for a cable.

The cattle and extra horses were driven across the river or forded across. Several trips were made by the ferry before all of the wagon train were across. All of his life, Will enjoyed telling about this experience.

After settling in Johnson County, Texas, Sterling met and married Jane's cousin, Virginia Ann Luttrell. In 1883, Sterling moved to Hunt County. Will was seven years old and getting big enough to work. Hosea Foster lived near the Hamblen family. He owned a cane mill. When the sorghum cane matured in the fall, it was cut and stacked near the mill.

G. G., Hosea's son, and Will became regular hands at the cane mill.

G. G. got up early and started the mill before going to school. He would push the stalks into the mill and as the cogs caught and crushed the cane, juice would squirt in every direction. G. G. had only one suit of clothes and he had them on. When he left for school, he had cane juice all over him and had to fight flies the rest of the day.

Will did not get to go to school. He continued to work at the mill. G. G. brought his books home at night and Will would study with him. He learned to read, write, and spell by studying the Blue Back Speller and McGuffey's Reader. He firmly believed that if a student learned phonics and spelled by syllables, he could spell any word written.

The Hamblen and Foster families migrated to the Texas Panhandle. The Fosters settled in Randall County. The Hamblens stopped at Claude in Armstrong County on November 8, 1890, [coming] by immigrant car over the Fort Worth & Denver railroad. All of the personal belongings, farming equipment, seed, cattle, and horses were loaded into the car. The boxcar was divided into partitions and boarded up with lumber. Lumber was also stored in the bottom of the car. Will, who was fourteen years old, rode in the car with the animals. The balance of the family came by passenger train.

After the car had been unloaded, the lumber was salvaged for use in building a house. The excrement from the animals had so discolored the lumber that no amount of lye soap and scalding water would remove the stains.

Sterling settled on a section of raw land south of Claude on the rim of the Palo Duro Canyon. Their first dwelling was a dugout. Because the family had grown, there was no place for Will to sleep. He spent that first winter sleeping in the wagon. He had grown so tall that his feet stuck out over the end. He never forgot that winter and how cold his feet would be.

One of Will's chores was to haul water for the stock and household use from a spring in the Palo Duro called Dripping Spring. An excavation was made at the spring to store the water, making it easier to fill the barrels by dipping the water in a bucket and pouring it into the several barrels in the wagon. Will's first dream of a road into the canyon began as he tried to maneuver his wagon from the floor to the rim.

In Hunt County, Will helped clear the land by digging up tree stumps. In Armstrong County, he broke the virgin sod with a walking plow pulled by a team of horses. This was so much easier than digging up tree stumps that he did not mind the work at all. The soil was rich and free of weeds. Underground moisture had not been depleted. Any thing planted grew and matured with very little effort on the part of the planter.

Sterling brought cotton seed from Hunt County. He planted and grew the first cotton to be grown in the Panhandle, which was strictly ranch country at that time. When the cotton had matured and the bolls had opened, Mrs. Adair of the JA Ranch and four of her cowboys rode by. She had never seen cotton growing and stopped at the field where the family was working. Today the cotton is stripped from the stalks by machine. When Will was a boy, the cotton was gathered by pulling the cotton out of the bolls by hand and storing it in a long cotton sack which the picker pulled behind him by use of a strap across his shoulder. When he had as much as he could drag, he slung the sack over his shoulder and carried it to the scales. There it was weighed and emptied into the cotton wagon.

Since there was no cotton gin in the area, the seed was picked from the cotton by hand. This was usually done after the evening meal before bed time. This was a family project, as a child was seldom too young to pick seed from cotton. Sterling had not planted a big cotton patch, but picking seed from the cotton and carding it into batts for quilts was a long, tedious task.

The Indian scare of 1891 is still talked about by the old-timers. The Luttrells lived about a mile from the Hamblens. Virginia glanced out the kitchen window at the Luttrell place. As she stared out the window, she wondered what in the world was going on at the Luttrells'. She could plainly see Molly Luttrell chasing a horse around the yard. He ran around the house with Molly right behind him. She sensed that there was an air of urgency in the yard activity. Molly caught the horse and came flying across the prairie at breakneck speed. Virginia ran out to meet her.

"Molly, what in the world is the matter?"

"The Indians are coming," gasped Molly.

"What do you mean?"

"The Indians are coming, they are tearing up the railroad track, killing women and children and burning houses," she screamed. "What in the world are we going to do?"

"Let's go to the Sebastions."

"I'll go get my family."

Virginia ran back into the house and told her oldest daughter to get a horse quickly and ride into the canyon for her father. Molly raced home to get her family together. Will and his father were in the Palo Duro cutting fence posts. They saw the girl flying toward them as fast as her horse could run. As she approached her father, she began to cry in frightened sobs.

"What is the matter?" her father asked in concern.

"The Indians are coming. They are killing every one. Mama and Aunt Molly are going to the Sebastions'. Mama said for you to come right home," she wailed.

Her father did not seem to be concerned. "Whoever heard of Indians coming in the daytime."

He and Will went home. Sterling saddled a horse and rode into Claude to find out whether or not the rumor was true. Will hitched a team to the wagon. Virginia gathered her children and the belongings she was taking with her and put them in the wagon. They drove toward the Sebastions'. Will's sister was still hysterical. She kept calling to Will between sobs:

"Drive up, Will; drive up, Will!"

When they arrived at the Sebastions', many of their neighbors were already there. The women and children were put in the dugout. The wagons were drawn into a circle and the horses driven inside. The men stationed themselves at windows in the house. One of the children was three days old. One of the women was expecting any day. One of the children had membranous croup and was doctored throughout the night with sugar saturated in coal oil. The dugout was crowded and only the small children were allowed a place to sleep. The night passed without incident. About midmorning, Sterling returned and told the men that the Indian scare had been a false alarm. Someone had misread the message coming over the teletype.

When Will was sixteen years old, his father told him that he was old enough to get out and make his own way. He found a job with a Mr. Turner, who had five girls and no boys. When Sterling learned that Mr. Turner had all girls and no boys, he told Will that it was not a proper place for him to work and made him find another. From that time on, Will was his own man.

Jobs were hard to find, and in the ranch country it was bronc riding and cowpunching. Will's first real employer was Henry Dye. His wife, Willie Ida, had been struck by lightning while they still lived in Hunt County. The lightning melted the tacks in her shoes and burst open her fingers. Two years later, she lost her eyesight, but Willie Ida was a pioneer. Losing her eyesight did not break her spirit. She was an immaculate housekeeper and would make the children's clothes after every one was in bed since she could not use a light. Henry took Willie Ida to see her relatives in Hunt County. Before they returned, Will and the boys cleaned the house. She dragged her feet as she walked across the floor and smiled as she said: "The floor is clean, isn't it?"

Will would never have thought that he would sit in a chair and let a blind woman go to the well and carry water to the house. Ranch work began early in the morning and quit late at night. The men were so tired when they came in that they would let her carry in the water. Henry Dye made a lasting impression on Will and helped to mold his character. Will was honest; if he gave you his word you did not need a written contract. He was hard-working, loyal to his family and friends, and most generous with his time and means in helping his neighbors.

Will worked for several different men in the Panhandle. He became expert at breaking horses. He was six feet, six inches tall. When he hooked his long legs over the back of a bronc, he was there to stay. There was a sadistic streak in Will's nature. He seemed to take pleasure in breaking the spirit of the animals he handled and making them bow to his will. When he rode a horse or hitched a wild team to a wagon, they were not allowed to stop until they were exhausted; then they found that they had a master.

Will's first job paid him fifteen dollars per month and board. Gradually, his jobs paid more money. In 1898, Will was hired by J. C. Carey to herd cattle on four sections of land in Moore County. He learned that land was available for filing so he filed on three sections of land near Dumas. While working for Mr. Carey, he began improvement on his own property.

In the months that followed, Will found time to ride the long miles back to the Palo Duro to visit his family. And a girl lived there.

Chapter 2

Almost hidden by the wild growth of grass, weeds, and shrubs, a room-size cave can be found in a recess of the Tule Canyon. Its floor is smooth from the tread of many moccasined feet. Remains of camp fires are still evident. The walls are stained with smoke and soot.

On its walls are crude drawings. One is of a horse. Another is a hand. Another is a group of wavy lines. A thunderbird or War Bird left a silent message. The picture of a man, standing aloof, with arms upraised, told a story to someone.

Many tribes wintered in the Palo Duro Canyon. This cave was a common meeting place of the chiefs. The most notorious of these chiefs was Quanah Parker. His most notorious visitor was José Piedad Tafoya, the Mexican comanchero.

Cynthia Ann Parker was nine years old when she was taken into captivity by the Comanche tribe. She never saw her people again and adopted her Indian family and Indian life wholeheartedly. She married a Comanche chief and bore two sons and a daughter.

A half-white boy in an Indian camp found that he had to be better than anyone else at anything. He must excel in sports, hunting, riding, or any other activity the children participated in. He had to earn their respect and their fear.

Quanah was mean. He was very intelligent, shrewd, and conniving, and he hated the white man.

When the cattlemen began settling in the plains of Texas, they brought in huge herds of cattle. Their remudas contained hundreds of horses. Mexico needed horses and cattle. The Indians needed blankets, beads, and cloth. An extensive trading business was established between the Mexicans and Indians. The leader of the Mexican comancheros was José Piedad Tafoya.

Although the Indians were supposed to be located on reservations in Oklahoma, they didn't stay there. They owned no horses and cattle of their own, so they raided the ranches, taking as many as they needed, trading them to José for the things they needed. It had been said that since the Indians had no business sense of value, a herd of three hundred cows would be exchanged for a bottle of whisky or a piece of bright-colored cloth.

Because of the numerous raids, the serious losses of the ranchers, the government was asked to send some soldiers in to contain the illicit trade. Several attempts were made to force the Indians back on the reservations but none were successful, until General Mackenzie took over the task.

He ran the Indians into the canyon, where they successfully eluded Mackenzie, following the canyon from Quitaque to the Tule. He was successful in capturing José. But José could not understand English. Each time that Mackenzie would ask José for information concerning the Indians, he would answer, "No sabe."

Losing his patience, yelling and cursing, Mackenzie told his men to prop up a wagon tongue and hang that so-and-so until he decided to talk. With a rope around his neck, and his feet barely touching the ground, José found that he could understand English better than he thought he could.

"Where is Quanah?"

Reluctantly, José told Mackenzie where the Indians were camped. Mackenzie and his men went after them. The ensuing battle was the last Indian battle to take place in America.[1] The Indians

---

1. The claim that the Battle of Palo Duro was the "last Indian battle to take place in America" falls short of accuracy, and the author's characterization of Indians is unflatteringly simplistic. It is also known that the conversation Quanah had regarding his multiple wives was not with President Roosevelt (who did become a friend of Quanah's). More rigorous research since the time of this book has yielded a fuller understanding of Native American life and culture (particularly the recapture of Quanah Parker's mother, Cynthia Ann, in December 1860). Excellent recent accounts may be found in T. R. Fehrenbach, *Lone Star: A History of Texas and Texans;* Paul R. Carlson and Tom Crum, *Myth, Memory, and Massacre: The Pease River Capture of Cynthia Ann Parker;* and Bill Neely, *The Last Comanche Chief: The Life and Times of Quanah Parker.*

fought fiercely, but they were fighting a lost cause. This site is still known as the Mackenzie Battle Ground. For years, it was rich in arrowheads, arrows, bullets, and other battle artifacts. If one is lucky, arrowheads and bullets may still be found.

General Mackenzie took all the horses to the head of the Tule Canyon and methodically killed the entire lot. This boneyard is still evident. He made the men, women, and children walk to Lawton, Oklahoma. Before the last Indian was out of the canyon, they had been walking three days.

Quanah evaded General Mackenzie and fled back to the reservation. He sent word to José that he would boil him in oil if he ever got his hands on him. José believed him and raced for the Mexican border. Once a very wealthy man, he died in obscure poverty.

In the Battle of Pease River, Chief Nocona and his wife, Cynthia Ann, tried to escape. She was on one horse with a two-year-old child in her arms. Nocona was on another with a fifteen-year-old girl on behind him. Sul Ross led the chase and killed Nocona. Cynthia Ann raced on. When Sul Ross captured her, he cursed himself soundly for nearly killing his horse trying to catch an old, dirty squaw. Her clothes were ragged and filthy dirty. Her face was so dirty, she really did look like a squaw except that she had blue eyes. Sul Ross thought he had found the missing Cynthia Ann. He sent for her uncle in Weatherford. When he arrived, Cynthia Ann apologized for her white parents. She was ashamed of them. She said she had an Indian mother and father. One of her sons died. Her infant daughter died. After about four years, Cynthia Ann died of a broken heart. She could not adjust to the life of the white man.

Quanah became the outstanding Indian of the day. He was chief of the allied tribes, Apache, Comanche, and Kiowa. He became the representative on Indian affairs for his people. He went to Washington and pleaded his cause before the president. On one occasion, he was in conference with President Theodore Roosevelt. Roosevelt was exhorting Quanah on the legality of having more than one wife. Quanah sat before him with bowed head.

"Quanah, it isn't right to have more than one wife."

"Ugh."

Left: Cynthia Ann Parker and daughter Prairie Flower, from a widely circulated photograph, circa 1869. Right: Quanah Parker, from a later widely circulated photograph.

"It is illegal. It is unconstitutional."

"Ugh."

"You are going to have to tell two of those women that they have to leave."

"Ugh." Quanah's face wore a worried look.

"Quanah, what are you going to do? Are you going to tell those women to leave?"

Quanah looked at President Roosevelt with troubled eyes. "Ugh. You tell 'em."

Quanah lived to be sixty-six years old. He was tall, erect, very proud, with graying hair and very dark skin. He never completely lost his resentment of the white man. His last recorded statement was this: "White man catch my mother. Take her back to her people. She try to run away. She no want to stay. She think of me . . . ."

Chapter 3

Will and Dan had been on the road since early morning. The air was fresh and clean. The prairie, green as far as the eye could see, was dotted with wildflowers and spires of yucca.

Will looked about him with a deep sense of well-being. Working for J. C. Carey was a lonely job, but it provided him with the means for improving his own land.

Will was going to see his parents and hoped to see a girl named Ada. Ada lived in the Palo Duro Canyon with her grandparents. Will did not get to see her very often. It was a long ride from his job to the Palo Duro. He always went one day and [come] back home the next.

Dan was the best quarter horse in the country. He had more cow sense than most men. Will had owned many horses and broken more than he had owned. He always said that he could tell what a horse was like by the way it held its ears. When Will saw Dan in the sale ring, he knew that he would make a good horse. Dan was just a yearling colt but he was full of fight. He was strong. His legs were good. He held his ears right.

Dan had loved running free on the range. He bitterly resented being in a sale ring, prodded with a stick and pushed around. It was a terrifying experience. Will was the highest bidder. A new life began for Dan.

Dan fought his rider furiously. He bucked. He sunfished. He tried to run out from under him. The weight on his back stayed there. The determination and skill of man overcame the determination and strength of the horse.

Dan could pace for hours, covering the miles easily and swiftly. He carried his head high; his ears pointed forward. His eyes glanced from side to side. He was watching for rattlesnakes and prairie dog holes. Will and Dan were enjoying the ride.

Since there were no roads crossing the Panhandle plains, they were following a drover's trail. One of the most famous of these trails is the Chisholm Trail, reaching from Abilene to Dodge City.[2] This trail can still be seen from the air. The trail Will was following crossed the Canadian River. Will knew the river well. He had crossed it many times. It was most dangerous after a rise. To the stranger, it was most hazardous. Heavy rains in New Mexico had caused the river to overflow. It had just reached a depth safe for crossing. Although it would rise swiftly, it also receded just as swiftly.

When Will was about a quarter of a mile from the river, he noticed that Dan had pricked up his ears. His head was pointed toward the river. Dan had heard something. Will soon heard the sound.

"Help! Help! Somebody help!"

The cries were those of a woman. He thought he heard a child crying. Urging Dan forward at a gallop, they soon reached the crossing. Mired in the bed of the river were two immigrant wagons. A man was whipping, cursing, and shouting at a team hitched to his wagon. A woman and child were on the other wagon. As the horses surged and scrambled for solid footing, the wagon sank lower. The muddy, rolling water was reaching for the wagon bed. The horses were falling, fighting and rearing in their terror.

Will urged Dan into the water. Dan knew that river. He had felt the tight sucking of the sand on his feet. He backed up, shaking his head and snorting his dislike. The firm pressure of knees in his side and the touch of spurs in his flanks told him that he would have to obey.

"Take it easy, boy. We'll make it. Steady, boy, steady."

Dan arched his neck. His ears were pointed and his eyes rolled. Carefully, lifting his feet high, he stepped into the water.

"I'll tie my rope to your wagon tongue and help you out. Let the horses settle down. We can get you out."

"Get your damned horse the hell out of here. I'll get out of this damned river myself."

Will watched the man whip his horses into a fighting, heaving mass, throwing the foaming water in all directions, only to sink lower

---

2. The author has confused the geography of the Chisholm Trail, which reached from southern Texas to Abilene, Kansas.

Drawing by Lynn Canafax

into the water.

"Lady, I will tie my rope to the tongue of your wagon. Hold the team firm until I tell you that I am ready."

"I will try. Please get us out of here." Her voice was filled with panic. The child began crying in terrified screams.

When Will told the woman that he was ready, Dan had taken up the slack in the rope. He bowed his neck; the muscles in his hind legs bulged as he strained against the weight. The woman whipped the horses and as they felt the easing of the wagon's pull from the sucking sand, they settled down to a steady, even draw.

Will and Dan reached the bank and dry solid ground. They turned back to help the man. The wagon was almost out of sight. Screams of terror were coming from the horses. They were fighting and heaving. But they were hitched to the wagon. The man was trying to cut the horses loose. Will tried to help him. The wet, muddy leather was too much for them to handle.

First, one of the horses pulled under, then the other. Will helped the man to the bank. They turned and looked back. The placid, flowing water was reaching for the sea.

Chapter 4

The first trail into the Palo Duro was made by the numerous herds of buffalo that roamed the great Staked Plains. They had a built-in engineering instinct that helped them find the path of least resistance.

Following the buffalo were the nomadic tribes of Indians that inhabited the area. They made their winter headquarters in the canyon. Artifacts and remains of campsites may be found in Mulberry Flat and the Tule.

In 1540, Coronado, thirty years old, set out with a group of men and horses to find Cibola, the fabulous Seven Cities of Gold. He entered the Texas Panhandle in a line from Tucumcari to Vega, then [traveled] southeast to the Palo Duro. His path crossed the site of the city of Canyon. The vast plains had no landmarks of any kind. He was depending upon Indian guides. He found that they were taking him away from the direction he wished to follow. Finding that he had been betrayed, Coronado bound his guide in chains. He [the guide] was later executed.

Coronado traveled by "needle" compass. This was achieved by filling a container, cup or can, or whatever. Very carefully, without breaking the surface tension, a needle was placed on the water. It would float and the magnetic pull of the north pole turned the point to the north.

Standing on the brink of the Palo Duro, he looked across the thirteen miles of smoky, blue haze that touched the tips of the hills and dipped into the valleys that he would have to cross.

Calling together thirty of his men, he followed the "needle" north to the opposite side. His trail from the Palo Duro crossed [what is now] the location of the courthouse in Claude, continuing north into Oklahoma and Kansas.

Cattle from the great herds on the Panhandle prairie found the buffalo trail. The cowboys and chuck wagon followed the cattle. Wagons carrying supplies and repair equipment made their way to the canyon floor along these trails.

Three hundred fifty-two years after Coronado stood on the brink of the Palo Duro, the first settlers in the Wayside community followed this same time-worn path.

Seventy years later, man walked on the moon.

In 1892, the Bradford, Fisher, and McSpadden families arrived in Claude by immigrant [railroad] car. The material possessions of each family, which included farming equipment, were loaded onto a wagon. They had one team of oxen, four horses, and two milch cows. After the wagons were loaded, the families began their journey to the south in search of public land on which they could file.

The traveling across the prairie was without incident. It was another matter when they reached the rim of the Palo Duro Canyon. They stopped and stared, unbelieving, at the great rift in the earth's surface. The blue haze hanging low did not hide the hard, rough terrain.

The back wheels of the wagons were chained to the brake box. This prevented them from rolling and acted as a brake in controlling the speed of their descent down the steep grades. Urging their teams forward, they began the arduous and exhaustive task of following a dim trail to the canyon floor.

The slow-plodding oxen were not easily excited. They felt their way over the rocks and around boulders, mesquite, and cedar. Slowly, they made their way, holding the wagon back when it threatened to roll headlong down the canyon wall.

The horses were more temperamental. A wagon riding their back sides and rocks rolling from under their feet made Mr. Bradford's team run away. Fortunately, the wagon did not overturn and the horses were halted. Mr. Bradford changed places with his son-in-law John Fisher and drove the oxen thereafter.

Upon reaching the canyon floor, the families met with a new experience. They found that they would have to cross the river. The water was shallow and barely flowing. How peaceful it looked. The children had great fun wading. The horses and oxen were given a chance to rest before starting for the rim on the south. Nowhere is the quicksand so treacherous and misleading as in the Canadian and the tributaries of the Red River. The families, inexperienced in quicksand, made the crossing without mishap. However, it was an experience that those who made the crossing related in horror and [they] forever after held quicksand in great respect.

Climbing to the rim required many rest stops. In many instances, the path had to be cleared ahead of the teams. Upon reaching the canyon floor, the wheels [were] unchained. Pulling a loaded wagon to the rim was quite different from riding it down. When the flat tableland called the Park was reached, both man and beast were exhausted.

The Park was a strip of land about three miles long and a mile wide, between the Palo Duro and Happy Canyon. Happy Canyon was a source of water supply from springs. The tableland provided pasture for the two cows, oxen, and horses. The families settled on this strip of land, building dugouts and breaking out a few patches of ground for gardens.

Soon, other squatters arrived, among them Old Mother McGehee and her children. Old Mother was a widow, and she planned to settle in the new country with each of her children filing on land. All of the families moved from the Park to open range country south of Happy Canyon. They filed on land throughout the area and became the foundation of the community which followed.

The parents became concerned about their children's education. In 1893 they took up contributions and bought enough lumber to build a one-room building. Mr. McSpadden gave the land for the schoolhouse and a cemetery.

Fearing that the building would be blown over by the strong winds which swept across the prairie, its builders braced it on each side with cedar logs reaching from the eaves to the ground. There were only a few students, and their favorite pastime at noon and recess was running up and down the cedar logs like squirrels. Only one casualty resulted. One of the boys, not quite so sure-footed as the others, fell off the log and broke his arm.

The school needed a name. Old Mother McGehee named the school Beulah for Beulah McSpadden, the first child born in the new

community. Sally McGehee, daughter of Old Mother, was the first teacher.

Only the strong in heart, soul, and body survived the hardships of those early days. There were no doctors or dentists. Much of the medicine was home-grown herbs, mustard plasters, and coal oil. Every one used coal oil for light. If anyone was injured, he was doctored with coal oil. If a child took cold, he was doctored with coal oil. Mustard plasters were used for chest colds, which too often developed into pneumonia. They were supposed to irritate the skin and draw out the infection. Nearly everyone spent several days peeling off afterwards.

Living conditions were especially harsh on small children and babies. Small graves dot the prairies. Sometimes there would be a large grave and beside it a tiny one. The first person to be buried in the new cemetery was a child named Bertie Bradshaw. Mrs. Bradford came from a medical family, so she had more knowledge of treating the sick than most of the pioneers. She treated Bertie with everything within her knowledge. But Bertie had diphtheria, a disease fatal to children. Membranous croup was another disease dreaded by all parents and almost surely fatal to small children. Pneumonia was feared by young and old. It knew no exceptions.

A fence was built around Bertie's grave to keep the cattle from trampling it down. This fence was left intact after the cemetery grounds were enclosed by a strong barbed and hog wire fence. Only in the last few years was it removed.

The second grave was that of a baby born premature. The father put the small body in a box and buried it in the cemetery. There was no marker, only a wooden slab which has rotted away. When Will and Ada lost their first child, born premature, Will carried it in a box by horseback from the canyon floor to the cemetery. It is presumed that he and a friend buried the child without other assistance.

One story told by the Tiptons, who lived on the canyon floor, concerned a family stopping at their home to rest on their way to the south rim. The baby was sick and cried a great deal. The father whipped the child. The mother seemed to be too frightened to interfere. After the family had passed through the area, a small grave was found beside the road. No one tried to find proof, but [it] was accepted fact that the father had killed the child by whipping it.

Mail delivery did not come to the Beulah community for several years. The mail was carried from Claude to Silverton by way of Beverly, [where there was] a small store owned by a Mr. Lemmons. The mail for anyone in that area was left at the store. Anyone going in that direction picked up the mail for all of his neighbors.

In 1893, a pickup station was established at a JA gate. This station was called Cornelia. In about 1896 or 1898, Mr. Bradford had the first post office in his home. He had a two-room house. In the front room, he put a chuck box. He divided it into little compartments and labeled each compartment for the person whose mail would be picked up there. Mrs. Bradford lined the chuck box with newspapers, making it clean and neat. The door to the chuck box could be closed and locked. There was no money involved. The Bradfords just did this for the benefit of the community.

The post office needed a name. Mrs. Bradford and her daughter Cassie sent in three names to the Post Office Department. They replied that since there was already a post office named Beulah, they would have to select another.

One of the names submitted by Mrs. Bradford was Wayside, a name taken from the Bible since the community seemed to be a place by the wayside. The Post Office Department chose the name Wayside, which became the official name for the community. The first mail carrier was W. F. Madison. He carried the mail from Happy to Wayside. He developed pneumonia due to exposure and died. His son A. F. was an early day mayor of Amarillo.

In 1905, Will bought the section of land owned by Mr. Bradford for one dollar per acre. The post office was moved to the center of the community to the home of William David McGehee. The carrier would make the trip from Happy one day and go back the next. He traveled in a buggy unless the weather and roads were too bad; then he traveled by horseback.

Curtis McGehee built and opened a store in the community. The post office was moved into an official building. A small corner of the store was divided off from the store proper and became the post office. Curtis was the first postmaster. He sold the first money order to Ruby McGehee in 1910.

When the postal inspector first visited Curtis, he almost panicked. The inspector was a government official. He had heard so many stories about how tough they [the officials] were and how some guys had been sent off to jail. Curtis got out his books, poured his money out of coffee cans and fruit jars. Most of it was pennies, but there were a few dimes and nickels. Much to his relief, he checked out clean. He made about fifteen dollars per month commission.

W. I. Lane, a former JA cowboy and husband of Bessie McGehee Lane, took over the management of the store. He went to Clarendon and bought a two-cylinder Maxwell [automobile] and drove it across the Palo Duro. The road was somewhat better than the first travelers found it. He made it fine going down the north wall and crossed the river with no trouble. His trouble began when he started out the south side. He had to get a team of mules to pull him out.

W. I. Lane carried the mail for several years. Bessie was the postmistress. Her son Joyce inherited the job and is postmaster at the present time. During the sxity-some-odd years of the history of the post office, there have been five postmasters who were members of Old Mother's family.

Chapter 5

The freighting of supplies and building material became a business with the influx of settlers during the development of the plains country. There were no roads. There were no fences. There was an abundant supply of water in the many playa lakes, and rich native prairie grass furnished feed for the horses.

S. P. Hamblen, Will's father, ran a freight line from Amarillo to Plainview and Roaring Springs. He worked eight head of horses, hitched tandem in pairs. He used one line fastened to the bridles of the lead team with check reins. When he jerked the line once, the lead team turned left. When he jerked it twice, the lead team turned right.

Another freighter who left his footprint on the pages of history was James Artemas Baker. In 1889, he arrived in Amarillo by way of the Fort Worth & Denver. He bought five acres of land from Judge Plemons for a hundred dollars. This land was in the area of the present location of the [ASARCO copper] smelter. It was near Wild Horse Lake and the first settlement, called Ragtown.

Leaving Amarillo, he traveled south, across uncharted plains. There were no roads, only cattle trails. The vast expanse of waving buffalo grass reached to the horizon.

He filed on 640 acres of land in Floyd County, then went back to Hamilton for his wife and children. Their son, Francis, was one month old when they left Hamilton by covered wagon for their new home.

He loaded household goods, farm implements, food, seed, and other commodities on two wagons. He had several hundred dollars in gold coins in the bottom of a trunk. He had one yoke of oxen, two mules, one mare and colt, and a few cows.

James and his wife, Alice, were on the road three weeks. Again, James Baker followed uncharted roads. They saw few people along the way and when they arrived at their new home, there were fewer than twenty people in the county.

After settling his family in a dugout and the two wagons, James A. Baker made his first freighting trip to Amarillo for lumber and supplies. This was the first of many such trips.

In 1895, James bought eighty acres of land, built a dugout and two-room house, and opened the first store in Lockney. The family lived in one room and the store was in the other. He traded supplies for anything offered for sale. There was very little money exchanged. No one had any money.

Some of the old ledgers show skunk, badger, and wolf hides at fifty cents each. Cow hides brought one dollar per hide. Chickens were ten cents apiece, and eggs were about the same. Buffalo bones brought five dollars per load. All of these commodities were freighted to Amarillo and sold.

Francis Baker began his freighting experience at the age of four and a half years. At the age of eight, he drove the freight wagon, along with other freighters, to Amarillo, peddling his wares and buying supplies. Francis knew the way; he knew where the water holes and rest stops were.

Some of the freighters from Lockney were Daff Griffith and his sons Jim, Theo, Roy, and Fred, with two six-horse outfits. Jim Thornton, Bob Farnsworth, and Sam Mills were also freighters. Francis liked to travel with Sam Mills. He had a doghouse built onto his wagon and fitted with a bachelor stove, bedding, and plenty of cow chips.

Walter Posey, Jules Snodgrass, Harry Snodgrass, and C. Surginer were freighters from Floydada.

R. M. Irick, Charley Durham, and Light Knight were freighters from Plainview. Light Knight worked Percheron horses, the largest horses on the road. R. M. Irick worked eight head of the best mules on the road.

Clay Holt was from Silverton. P. E. Cowart operated a country store in Silverton and freighted his supplies.

During the winter, the farmers went to the Palo Duro and cut fence posts. They traded them to James Baker for supplies. He piled them up until he had four wagonloads, then he hauled them to Lubbock for sale. On the way back he and Francis picked up dry, bleached bones.

Cow hides were stored until he had two wagonloads. As farming developed, the commodities purchased by the Baker store changed. He began dealing in milo heads, oats, kaffir, and other grains. If he had large loads, James took his purchases right on into Amarillo. Often, he was able to dispose of them locally.

Alice Baker worked right alongside her husband. She cared for the children. She operated the post office and store. In the absence of her husband, she assumed full responsibility of the home. And she had babies: nine of her children were born at Lockney, making a total of twelve, six boys and six girls. Alice and James Baker taught their children to work and assume responsibility at an early age.

James Baker charted the first route to Amarillo by way of Happy Hollow. The Curry family had established a home with a windmill and tank to furnish water. Happy Hollow was about one and one-half miles east of the present location of Happy. They built a wagon yard with plenty of horse lots and stalls and a camp house for the freighters. When the Santa Fe [Railroad] constructed a branch line from Amarillo to Slaton, Happy Hollow moved to the railroad and dropped the "Hollow." The farm where the Curry family operated the wagon yard is still called the Curry place.

In 1896, the homesteaders began moving in and putting up fences, which changed the routes of the freighters. The trails were forced to go around fields and pastures. A Mr. Ballard established a wagon yard with a good camp house and corrals for the horses about five miles southeast of the present location of Happy. He supplied mules for the mail stage line, feeding and caring for the team left by the change which occurred twice a day. Often, as many as a dozen freighters would be camped for the night.

Illness was the only valid excuse for one of the Baker children to miss a day of school. When Alice looked out the post office window and saw her son Francis standing on the porch at nine o'clock in the morning, she didn't say a word. She reached for the leather strap hanging just inside the door and proceeded to use it with great diligence.

Then she asked Francis why he was home from school. Francis told her that the teachers had closed the school. There was no money. They had not been paid for the month before, and there was no money for the present. She asked how much was needed to keep the school in operation until the end of the term. She promised them the needed amount and kept her promise.

In 1914, the frame building that housed the Baker store burned. James built the brick structure that stands today.

In 1915, a man brought in a calf hide. James handled it with bare hands. In three days he had succumbed to blackleg, a new disease that was sweeping through the cattle. There was no serum for inoculation. After the death of her husband, Alice continued to run the store, with the help of her children.

For fifty years, Alice Baker operated the store in the same manner as did her husband. She never refused credit to anyone. She never lost an account. She never asked for a note or a mortgage. She never threatened a lawsuit. The old ledgers show the sale of bacon, flour, and sugar to "One Legged Man." Another sale is listed as "Stranger." Stamps and money orders were sold and charged to the buyer's account. Subscriptions to the *Dallas Semi-Weekly News, Youth's Companion,* and other periodicals were sent in and charged to the subscriber's account.

Merchandise freighted consisted of anything the people needed. As the country developed, the needs grew more varied. Lumber, barbed wire, hardware, dry goods, flour, bacon in hundred-pound gunny sacks, canned goods, dried fruit in fifty-pound boxes, round cheese in ten-pound blocks, sugar in hundred-pound bags, coal oil in fifty-gallon drums, molasses in fifty-gallon wooden barrels, honey in five-gallon tin containers, men's clothing, shoes, boots, vinegar in fifty-gallon wooden barrels, pins, needles and thread, bolts of dry goods since women's ready-to-wear was unheard of. The women also made their own bonnets.

May 14, 1971, the Floyd County Historical Society installed a historical marker on the front of the building which houses the Baker Mercantile and [is] operated by Dimple Baker McGavock. James Artemas Baker and his wife, Alice, founded a business that has continued to be operated by a Baker for seventy-seven years.

[Text of historical marker in Lockney, Floyd County, Texas:]

J. A. BAKER STORE

Opened 1894. One of the Texas South Plains' oldest mercantile houses still owned by founding family. James Artemas Baker (1859–1917), founder of this store and town of Lockney, was born near Dallas and lived in Hamilton from 1879 to July 1890, when he moved here. Acting postmaster in 1893 and serving by appointment from 1894 to 1901, he freighted and, with the help of his wife Alice, ran this store, selling hardware, sundries, dry goods, groceries. Town also relied on Baker's store safe for banking in the early days. After the frame building burned, this structure was erected in 1914. (1971)

Chapter 6

"Ladies to the center and back to the bar.
Gents to the center with a right-hand-star.
Back to the left and don't get lost.
Pass your gal and take the next.

The ladies swing in and the gents swing out.
Break in the center, and every one swing.
Now, allemande-left with that left-hand gal.
And back to your new gal and promenade."

Will and Ada had been riding in silence as their horses felt their way down the rocky path leading to the headquarters of the JA Ranch. The night was still and quiet. Velvet shadows clothed the sides of the cliff and around the bushes and trees. High overhead, the man in the moon had a benevolent look on his face as he watched the scene.

Far in the distance, they heard the lonesome cry of a coyote. Soon, they heard an answering call. They heard the soft whir of wings as birds of the night flew overhead. The creaking of saddles and soft clop of horses' feet did not drown out the melodious voice of the caller, as dancers executed the "Texas Star."

The riders smiled at the sound of music and fun. They looked forward with keen anticipation to meeting old friends and enjoying an evening of fellowship.

The date was the evening before May 1. As sure as the sun rose in the east and set in the west, the JA annual round-up began May 1. The boys came in from Camp Pleasant, Tule Camp, Stinkhole Camp, and the many other camps scattered over the six-hundred-section ranch. Will was not a regular JA ranch hand. He worked for them occasionally, breaking horses or helping for a short time with round-up. But when the JA's gave the boys a dance, every one within riding distance attended.

The fiddler was Arthur Howard. The guitar player was Jimmy Rogers. The caller was Bole Mayo. As Will and Ada neared the huge building where the dance was held, they could hear the stomp of boots and the jingle of spurs. An occasional whoop of exhilaration came from a dancing cowboy.

The dancing lasted until daybreak. The musicians put away their instruments. The jingle of spurs on dancing feet became a soft tinkle as the men went about their tasks. The girls went home barefooted, since they had danced the soles off their shoes.

Will and Ada mounted their horses and rode back up the canyon wall. The glamour had gone from the scene. It was daylight and to the cowboy, the scene was stark and hard. When they arrived at Ada's home, Will bade his girl good-bye, then began the long, lonesome ride to his spread between the fork of the Big Blue and Little Blue rivers.

As Will and Ada turned toward home, the JA ranch hands walked into the rising sun. The hour for light hearts and gaiety had passed. The serious business of spring round-up was beginning.

For days, preparation had been under way. Needed repairs had been made. Materials and equipment had been stocked. Mitch Bell, the wagon boss and cook, had supervised the chuck wagon. Flour, sugar, potatoes, dried beans, canned peaches and tomatoes, coffee, and pots and pans were stored in the wagon.

On a second wagon, known to all ranch people as the hoodlum wagon, were the boys' bedrolls, water barrels, and tools for miscellaneous repair. The straw boss was in charge of the hoodlum wagon.

Each man furnished his own bedroll. It consisted of two or three blankets or quilts and a tarp. The tarp kept the bed off the damp ground and gave its owner protection when it rained. If the bedroll got wet, it was spread out in the sun to dry. The bedrolls became quite pungent, since they were not washed until fall. Some of the men were regular employees, while others were employed for the round-up only.

The wagon boss, or cook, could always expect to have visitors at mealtime. He could have from thirty to forty people, both men and women, to feed. As the chuck wagon made its way across the range, former ranch hands, businessmen, and farmers found an opportunity to eat at least one meal with the boys.

Three times a day, the men had biscuits, meat, and potatoes. Each day a beef would be killed and dressed. Since there was no way of preserving the meat, what could not be used was given to the nesters or whoever could use it, and the next day another would be killed. If there was no one to use the meat, it was left on the prairie for the coyotes.

Huge pots of coffee hung from tripods. The taste could be bitter and the strength strong, but it was hot and relaxing. The greatest hardship on both man and beast was a shortage of water. The stock did without. The men ate canned peaches and tomatoes.

Everyone catered to the cook. No one played tricks on him. A handout in the middle of the afternoon helped a guy make it until night. A cook could make the biscuits hard and flat, the meat raw, and the beans hard. When he called "come and get it before I throw it out," they came because he might do just that. It was a long time between meals.

The straw boss drove the hoodlum wagon. He served as cook when the wagon boss was ill or needed to be elsewhere. He killed and dressed the beef. He had to keep a supply of firewood at all times. If they were camped in or near the breaks, the firewood was mesquite or cedar. If they were on the prairie, it was cow chips. He went to the nearest town for supplies. Since the horses must be watered from the water barrels, keeping a supply of water could be quite a chore.

Each ranch raised its own horses. The best ones were kept for ranch work, the culls shipped out. Homesteaders made extra money breaking these wild horses during the winter months. To those of us who handle horses today, those horses were still wild when turned back to the owners. The cowboy knew that when he rode on one of those horses, he would have to ride him good if he stayed on.

When the horses were brought in from winter pasture, they were raw, rugged, and sinewy. Each man was issued a string of horses numbering from ten to twenty animals. If the range was dry and the grass short, they would have about twenty animals. If the grass was good, they would have about ten. The horses were not fed; they were turned loose to graze and forage for themselves. Each animal was used a half day then turned out. He would not be used again for about a day and a half. Again, this practice varied according to range conditions. The range horse was as sturdy and rugged as the cowboy. Many times he was not pretty to look at, but he knew cattle. He knew cattle as well as the cowboy did.

When the remuda was brought in, each horse hoped he would not be the one chosen to work that day. He would try to get into the middle of the milling huddle, lowering his head to miss the lariat loop. The cowboy knew all of these tricks. Swinging his lariat over his head, he would let the loop sail lazily out over the bobbing, milling heads. It would fall unerringly over the head of its intended victim. After being saddled and bridled, the horse would get the cunning idea that he would just dump the aggravating weight. This never worked either. If a horse turned out to be raunchy, he was given to Wiatt Hiesler, one of the regular JA cowboys; like Will, he never straddled a horse that he could not ride.

Annual round-up meant long hours of hard riding. It meant getting up early and going to bed late. It meant going into out-of-way places looking for cattle. A smart cow could hide with her calf. She had been through round-up. It meant branding all of the calves and the older stock that had been missed earlier. It meant days of lonely riding. It was a way of life. The horse was the most important factor in this way of life and without him, man's work could not function.

After going through his daily routine of trying to buck his rider off, the horse would settle down. He always kept his eyes on the cow or calf he was after. He could follow the animal through a herd without losing him. If the cow or calf laid his ears back, he was going straight ahead. If the animal swerved to the left, so did the horse. If he swerved to the right, so did the horse. A good horse could turn on a dime. When the lariat sailed out over the head or feet of a cow or calf, the horse stopped, backed up until the rope was tight, then held the animal until the cowboy signaled that he could let him up.

When annual round-up had been completed, about 15,000 calves would have been branded and worked. All of the cattle to be sold were driven to the shipping pens at Clarendon. Some went to slaughterhouses in the east and some went to feeders in the Midwest.

With all of the activity surrounding round-up, there were very few

Top left: Cowboys and visitors dining at the chuck wagon of C. T. Ward, Canyon City, Texas. Center: Chuck wagon with tent used on ranches in early days. Bottom: R. M. Irick's big freight outift moves a two-story home from Dimmitt, in Castro County, to Plainview, in Hale County, some forty miles, without mishap. (From contemporary Texas newspapers, uncredited in original book.)

major accidents. Maybe it was because the boys grew up respecting horses and cattle. A greenhorn didn't last long in the hard rugged life. If he did make good, he earned the respect of his fellow man.

When an accident did happen, the men were laconic in their humor. A program of upgrading their stock was instigated by the JA. They imported some high-grade, registered bulls. While [the men were] handling the bulls, one of them charged Wiatt, knocking his horse from under him. Wiatt jumped free and started running for a slight arroyo. He fell into the ditch as the bull raked his back sides. As he raced by, the bull stumbled and fell. Mitch Bell, seeing that Wiatt was unhurt, sardonically remarked, "Wiatt, that is one of our best bulls. I wish you would be more careful."

Henry Morgan was a good, experienced cowboy. He saddled his horse and rode out on the range. When the riderless horse came back to camp, the boys rode out looking for him. When they found him, there was not much left to bury. His foot had caught in the stirrup of his saddle, spooking his horse. No one knew whether the horse stumbled and fell or what happened for Henry to get caught like that. He had been dragged through cacti and mesquite. The spears of bear grass had cut like a knife.

Claude Hamblen became enraged at his horse and proceeded to kick the daylights out of him. The horse didn't mind too much, but Claude broke his big toe. He knew that if he took his boot off, he would never get it back on again. He wore the boot for three months. The toe healed and the bone was straight.

A young man just beginning his career as a cowboy met disaster while crossing a rain-swollen creek. His horse became frightened at the water and quicksand. Plunging and rearing, he threw the boy into the water. Before help could reach him, he had drowned.

Each man owned at least one horse. He furnished his own saddle,

Will Hamblen on horseback, as a young man (Hamblen family collection)

bridle, and lariat. He wore good boots, spurs, and chaps. The leather chaps were a protection against weather, horns of cattle, mesquite thorns, and underbrush. After the round-up was finished, the men gathered their gear, received their pay, then went their separate ways. Some of the regular boys went to winter camps on the range. Some of them drifted on. Others went to homes on their own land.

The colorful era of the cowboy has been replaced by progress and invention. Old-timers dwell with nostalgia on days gone by. It was survival of the hardy for men, women, and animals. As long as we have artists and writers, progress and invention will never erase completely the history of the sturdy men and women who built the Panhandle.

Chapter 7

WIATT HEISLER PRACTICALLY GREW UP ON THE JA RANCH. His father, Charles F. Heisler, worked on the ranch for thirty-two years. The father loved the ranch. He loved every activity that went into its operations. He had worked at every job connected with the running of a huge spread.

He had watched the ranch grow from a small holding to a corporation. He had watched it grow from a few hundred head of cattle to several thousand. He had watched it grow from a few sections of land to hundreds of sections. He expected to be a part of its operation as long as he lived.

One day, he received a letter from the ranch manager, Mr. Hobert. Charles Heisler opened it with no premonition as to what it contained. Coldly and brusquely, the letter informed him that because of his age, he would no longer be working for the JA.

It would have been easier for him to take if Mr. Hobart had told him in person. The announcement broke his heart. He died soon after.

Wiatt became general ranch hand in 1907. His salary was twenty-five dollars per month. This was increased to thirty dollars, then thirty-five dollars, and his highest salary was seventy-five dollars. He, too, had worked at every activity connected with running a big spread. He was straw boss for seven years. He worked for the JA for several years after he married, then became a stockman and farmer in the Wayside community.

Young Will Hamblen, drawing by Lynn Canafax

Chapter 8

Will Hamblen liked girls. He was acquainted with most of the girls in the Panhandle area. He called upon several and was a little serious about two or three, but his eyes always strayed back to Ada. Her curly black hair, her soft brown eyes, her lithesome figure inherited from her Indian ancestry, made her the most attractive of all the girls in Will's eyes.

Will was considered to be a good catch by all of the parents with marriageable daughters. He owned three sections of land in the fork between the Big Blue and Little Blue rivers. He was accumulating cattle and horses. He was a hard worker. His character above reproach, his clean-cut features, and his six-foot-seven-inch stature made him a man of distinction wherever he went. Parents praised him to their daughters and held him as an example of fine young manhood to their sons.

Ada was never without admirers. Most of the young men within riding distance had called upon her. One of her admirers became so positive that he was winning her hand, that he built a dugout with the expectation of taking her there as his bride.

Will did not write many letters, but when he wrote to Ada, telling her of his love and closing with this statement: "Where ever you are, that is where I want to be," he won her heart. She treasured this letter for many years; eventually it was lost.

Will was not afraid of man nor beast. But when he thought of facing Ada's grandfather, a white-headed, white-bearded, stern Baptist minister, his heart quailed. He worried needlessly. Grandfather Tipton was most happy to have his only granddaughter marry such a promising young man. Will rode back to his ranch, gay of heart and free of spirit. The sky had never been so blue. Although the prairie was brown from the frost and the wind was cold, it was a beautiful world. He even crossed the Canadian [River] without mishap.

Will and Ada became engaged in the fall of 1899. Their wedding day was set for October 16, 1900. Will went to see Ada several times during this year, but most of his time was spent improving his land. He had filed on the land and, to meet government regulations, he had to make certain improvements. During this time, he built their first home.

Practically all of the early Panhandle settlers lived in dugouts. Dugouts provided excellent protection from the terrible blizzards that swept across the plains in the winter and were cool in the summer. Anyway, there wasn't any lumber to build houses. Will did not dig a dugout. His house was dug out of the hard, clay cliff. It was large enough for two rooms. He shored up the ceiling to keep the dirt from sifting down. He built the front and outside wall of logs, plastering the cracks between the logs with clay.

The dwelling had one outside door, and each room had one window. A strip of canvas served for a door. Cloth covered the windows. Will built a fireplace but he also had a bachelor type stove.

Ada spent the months of her engagement filling her hope chest. She crocheted yards of lace. She embroidered pillowcases and dish towels. She embroidered dresser scarves and quilted quilts. Her grandmother and Will's half-sister, Effie, worked with her. These articles were a part of every household. It was the only way the women could beautify their bare, sparsely furnished homes.

Mrs. B. T. Johnson made Ada's wedding dress. It was of white cashmere. It had a tight-fitting basque waist and leg-o'-mutton sleeves. The yoke of the dress was trimmed with shirred ribbon bands, and the collar stood up, fitting close around the neck. The skirt was cut in many gores and very full.

Ada made her own petticoat. The material was white muslin. It was gathered at the waist. Beginning at knee length, ruffles reached to the ankle. These ruffles were trimmed with pin tucks and lace. The pin tucks were put in by hand, but the lace was machine-made. One day when she and Effie were working on the petticoat, Will arrived unexpectedly. The girls had the petticoat spread out on the bed. In confused embarrassment, the girls hurriedly gathered the yards of material, trying to get the garment out of sight.

Ada and Effie spent the week before the wedding cleaning house.

They scrubbed the pine floors with sand until they took on the color of gold. The windows were washed inside and out until they sparkled. They washed and ironed. They decorated the tops of the windows with sprays of lacy, fernlike asparagus, the red berries turned a brilliant scarlet by the early frost. Bows of white satin ribbon were used to hold the spray together. A centerpiece for the table was made of asparagus. While the girls were cleaning and decorating, Grand-

Will and Ada Hamblen, wedding-day portrait, 1900

mother Tipton was baking. She made the four-layer cake, decorating it with white icing. She baked pies and cakes and chicken and all of the things the early settlers had for company dinner.

Sunday, October 16, 1900, at four o'clock in the afternoon, Will and Ada were married. Ada was beautiful in her white dress. Will was handsome in his bright, shiny boots, his coat sleeves just a little short and his pants legs not quite long enough. Ada did not have a bride's bouquet, but she did have a gold wedding band. Grandfather Tipton performed the ceremony before a house full of close friends and relatives of both families. Grandpa Tipton did not believe in short wedding services. When he finished, Ada and Will were solidly married.

Ada and Will Hamblen hold children Nellie (at left) and Alfred in their laps, circa 1905 (Hamblen family collection)

All of the guests stayed to eat the sumptuous meal that had been prepared and to wish Will and Ada godspeed. When the guests had departed, Will and Ada began making preparations to go to their new home.

The next two years were hard and lonely ones for Ada. She had been raised by her grandmother and missed her sorely. After the loss of their first child, Will and Ada proved their land, then sold it and moved to the Palo Duro. Years later this same land was the center of the great oil discovery in the Panhandle.

During the time Will and Ada lived with her elderly grandparents, their son Alfred and daughter Nellie were born.[3] They then moved to the section of land Will had bought from J. H. Bradford.

---

3. Here they lived a in dugout on the west side of the Prairie Dog Town Fork of the Red River.

Chapter 9

The men had long since left to ride the range. Jo Ellen finished drying the breakfast dishes and put them away in the dish cabinet. She stepped outside the back door and into the yard. The chickens needed to be fed and watered. The cows must be turned out to pasture.

The air was unusually still. The birds were not singing. At this hour of the day, jackrabbits and cottontails were usually frolicking about. There were no rabbits. She went about her morning chores, occasionally casting an uneasy glance at the clear, blue sky.

A light, gray haze hung in the west. Must be a storm brewing, she thought. There was nothing to indicate a storm, but then, in the Panhandle, that didn't mean anything.

The rank prairie grass was better than it had been in several years. The cattle would winter good. Her glance took in the stack of hay which would take care of the cattle when snow was on the ground. She looked at the big stack of cedar posts to be used in building more fences. She had enjoyed going to the canyon for posts. She would pack a big lunch, and they would spend the day cutting and trimming the cedar and hackberry trees into good posts. Hauling the posts out of the canyon was harder than cutting them. Sometimes, they just stacked the posts and left them to haul out later.

[Jo] Ellen looked at the gray haze in the west. It was higher, and there seemed to be some movement in it. An electric, uneasy feeling was in the air. With a troubled look in her eyes, she went back into the house.

About two hours later, she glanced out the kitchen window. Paralyzing fear held her motionless. The gray haze had become an ominous, black cloud. It was rolling and boiling and swirling in the sky. For miles, wicked, ugly yellow flames were reaching out hungrily.

Jo Ellen knew that the fire was moving swiftly. A prairie fire creates its own wind, and although it was still miles away, Jo Ellen had very little time. "What can I do? What shall I try to save?"

Soon she heard galloping horses and went out into the yard, as her husband, Jake, and his men jumped from their horses. "Get the broom, Jo Ellen. We need some tow sacks. Ralph, you hitch a team to the wagon, and fill some barrels with water. John, hitch a couple of horses to the plow and widen the fire guard. This one is bad. I am afraid it will jump."

Quickly and efficiently, the men went about their tasks. They worked silently. There was no need and no time for words.

"I am going to ride on, and you boys come as soon as you can. Jo Ellen, maybe you had better get the cows in the lot. We may need to kill one. If the fire comes this far, and you see that it is going to burn us out, get on your horse and get out of its path."

Jake raced toward the fire. He could feel the heat and knew this was the worst that he had ever seen. It was going to be hard to contain. He knew that men along its path were fighting desperately. He knew that men in front of it would be gathering to help stop its depredation. As he neared the inferno, he could see the action along its border. Men were swinging wet sacks along its edge. Others had brooms, wetting them in barrels of water, sweeping at the flames. The fire was five miles wide. All they could hope to do was keep it from spreading wider.

Jim Christian roped a cow, and quicker than any man there, he had her skinned and ropes tied to the legs of the wet hide. He tied one end of the rope to the horn of his saddle, while Jake tied the other rope to his saddle horn. Jim raced in front of the fire. Jake raced the burnt side, dragging the wet cow hide through the flames until the ropes burned and the horses' feet were singed. The fire raged on.

Jo Ellen watched the fire. It danced along its edge, leaping into the air when it found a bunch of bear grass, shrieking and laughing in devilish glee at the efforts of man. The birds and rabbits knew disaster was in the air. If only man possessed the instinct God has given birds and animals! She watched the roaring furnace creeping toward the fire guard. Was it going to hold?

Jake was fighting desperately. As Jim raced to a new breakthrough, his horse stumbled. Jim jerked him to his feet. A few more steps, and he stumbled again. Jim could not jerk him to his feet this time. Jim leaped free as his horse fell dead, bursting his heart as he gave everything he had.

She watched the stack of hay scorch. She watched the pile of fence posts ignite. She watched the fire race on.

Only one thing lay in the path of the fire. The Palo Duro Canyon, its steep, rocky walls covered with sparse tufts of coarse grass and stunted trees, did not produce fuel easy to burn. As the fire reached its rim, the flames weakened and died, sighing softly and moaning low.

Wearily, the men gathered up their tools and began returning to their homes. They turned their faces to the west. As far as the eye could see and reaching into New Mexico, the blackened strip of prairie sent up little spirals of smoke where a cow chip still smoldered or a mesquite was still live with embers. Lightning leaped from peak to peak in a dark, white-frosted cloud. It would be raining soon.

Chapter 10

As the community developed, there were more children to go to school. In 1909, with the help of state funds, a two-room-with-auditorium building was erected. The auditorium was used for classes during the week and church services on Sunday.

Mr. and Mrs. J. W. McCrerey had moved to Texas from Kansas. They had been quite active in their lodge. One of the annual customs was a community Christmas tree on Christmas Eve. Mrs. McCrerey led the community in a project that has continued to the present.

Each Christmas Eve, a huge tree was placed in the schoolhouse auditorium. For many years the tree was brought out of the Palo Duro. As long as a school was conducted in the community, the tree and program were held in the schoolhouse. When the school was discontinued, the tree and program were held in the community church.

For over sixty years, the Wayside community has observed Christmas Eve in this manner. No one can remember when it was not held for any reason. Although the attendance is not so large, and there are fewer children, this community practice has continued to the present time.

Decoration Day has been observed in the Wayside community since May 30, 1916. A program was given by the children, with Clara McClain McGehee playing the piano for singing. Generally, there was an honored guest who spoke on the occasion.

At the close of the program, the children were given bouquets of flowers to place on the graves. For years, all of the children wanted to put flowers on the tiny grave without a marker. Gradually, it became lost.

The observance of Decoration Day has continued to the present. Visitors attend the service from Cape Kennedy [now Canaveral], Florida, to the state of Washington. They come from New York to Los Angeles, California. It is a community reunion. It is a day of fellowship.

Chapter 11

Food was a source of concern for the early settlers in the Wayside community. It was a two-day trip to either Claude or Amarillo. If the return load was going to be heavy, they drove four head of horses. Quite often, the weather was extremely cold, making the trip most difficult.

The route to Amarillo crossed the Block pasture and what is now known as the Six Mile crossing. This crossing was considered a halfway station. Every one tried to make this campsite at night. It provided shelter and firewood, but more important, it was a place where friends and new acquaintances met. News of the area was exchanged and passed on.

Supplies for a year would be purchased, including clothing, material for sewing, farm repair [supplies], seed, and building material. Lumber for building was hauled from Amarillo. The road to Claude was too long and rough for such a heavy load.

The early settlers brought with them all the food that they could store. The Fishers brought dried peaches. Coming from a fruit country, they sorely missed the fruit in their diet on the plains.

When Sybil Fisher Willis was asked what did they have to eat, she replied, "We ate lots of cornbread."

When Curtis McGehee was asked the same question, he replied with a wry grin, "Well, we ate lots of jackrabbits. There were lots of antelope, too."

Spring gardens were put in as soon as possible. Garden seed was shared with neighbors. Farm seed was divided with those who needed it. Everyone helped each other, for no one had any money.

Mr. Bradford broke out about an acre of sod. He used a walking plow to make the furrows. Carrying the seed wheat in a bucket, he dropped the seed in the furrows, then covered it by dragging a springtooth harrow across the ground. Planted in the fall, the wheat grew to a good stand. Mr. Bradford let his cows graze on it all winter. In the spring it began to joint and make a head. Mr. Bradford and John McGehee, his friend and neighbor, were looking at the small plot of wheat. Turning to his friend, Mr. Bradford remarked, "John, this is going to be wheat country."

Soon everyone was planting small fields of wheat. They could get it ground into flour. Too, it made good chicken feed. Jim McGehee, John's brother, built a threshing machine for the wheat. No one knows what happened to the thresher.

The only fruit in the country grew wild in the Palo Duro. Plums, cherries, and grapes grew in abundance. The mustang grapes would peel the tongue quicker than a frozen wagon-wheel rim, but they made excellent jelly and wine.

Every one set out an orchard. Transient peddlers of fruit trees traveled through the country, making a sale at practically every residence. Peach trees were the most popular item.

Every family canned and preserved as much food as possible. Glass containers called fruit jars were first used in canning. The first jars had zinc tops lined with porcelain. A rubber ring was placed over the top of the jar and the top then screwed on.

Fruits and tomatoes were easy to can because of their acid content. They were brought to a boil, then while hot, poured into the jars. The jars were sealed with the rubber ring and zinc top.

Fruit jars are collector's items today. Collectors look for certain markings on the bottom of the jar. They look for color. They look for size. A three-quart jar is almost impossible to find. A half-pint jar is most rare. If a collector is lucky, maybe he can find a blue Monday jar.

Glass lids fastened with a clamp replaced the zinc lid. A rubber ring still had to be used to seal it. Today, you find these jars on the coffee table with candy in them.

Beef clubs were formed consisting of about ten families. Each man would take turns killing a beef. It was then divided among the other members. This way, they could have meat more often and use it up before it could spoil.

When steam pressure cookers came into use, more vegetables could be canned. Peas, beans, greens, and corn were the most popular. Corn was the hardest to keep. It took practice to can corn. Corn was so deceiving. It did not blow the lid off. It just sat there looking clean and beautiful. There is absolutely no smell that reaches to high heaven like that of spoiled corn. Neither was there anything more delicious than that of a jar of good, sweet corn.

One of the first crops planted by the early settlers was corn. When the corn ripened in the fall, the ears were pulled, shucked, and shelled. Every one worked at shelling the corn, even the smaller children. This was done by rubbing the kernels from the cob by hand. Using another cob to rub the kernels loose helped to protect the hands. After the corn was shelled, it was carried to a mill near Vigo Park and ground into meal. The cobs were saved for fuel.

About three hundred years ago, sorghum cane was discovered on the island of Jamaica. It was carried to Cuba and from there to Florida and Louisiana. The plant was improved by the selection of seed heads. This cane became popular in making sorghum cane syrup. The seed was brought to the Panhandle by the early settlers and was the main source of sweets.

The cane grew to six or eight feet tall. When it was mature and before frost could damage it, the cane was cut with a cane knife. It was stripped of its leaves and piled in ricks between the rows. The cane was then piled on a wagon and hauled to the mill. It could not be too long from the time of cutting until it was hauled to the mill or it would dry out.

Little children helped with the cane, too. They could strip the leaves and pile it between the rows.

The cane was loaded onto a wagon with four-foot sideboards. When they got to the mill, the cane was unloaded and placed between poles stuck in the ground near the mill. The cane mill was operated by a team of mules or horses. The bridle of the inside animal was fastened to a beam with a check rein. This kept them [the animals] walking in a circle. One of the children watched to see that they did not stop. As they walked, they pulled the gears that pressed the juice from the cane. The juice was caught in fity-five-gallon barrels. Sometimes these barrels were called hogsheads. When a barrel was full of juice, it was emptied into a pan. A fire under the pan brought the juice to a boil. After a period of time, the juice was drained into another pan, then another, then into a fourth pan, which was the final cooking of the syrup. It took fifty-five gallons of juice to make eight gallons of syrup. The crushed pulp was fed to the livestock.

Vats were made of adobe bricks. These bricks were made of mud and grass. They were dried, then built into a vat about four feet wide and six feet long. Grates were placed in the bottom of the vats to put the firewood on. A flue was put in one end. This caused a suction of air beneath the wood and out the flue. The same principle was used in building fireplaces. Metal pans were placed on the adobe structure. The fuel was logs cut in three- or four-foot lengths and fed into the adobe vat from the side opening. The hottest fire was under the first pan. When the juice began to boil, it was drained into a second pan. The juice had begun to thicken. The fire was still less hot. When it was drained into the fourth pan, it was cooked to the right consistency. The fire was a bed of coals, and required constant watching. The person watching the fire knew exactly how much heat was needed under each pan. When the syrup became the finished product, it was drained into wooden syrup barrels, usually containing eight gallons.

This syrup was, most of the time, the only sweet the family had. The wife learned by ingenuity to make do. She made cakes, pies, taffy candy, and molasses cookies from the syrup. Another delicacy made from the syrup was vinegar pie.

Sugar cane is a sort of the old sorghum cane. It is harvested the same way but propagated differently. At harvest time, the best sugar cane stalks are selected and heeled out during the winter. This is done by digging a long trench. The stalks are laid lengthwise in the trench, then covered with dirt. About the middle of March, the stalks are uncovered. Each joint will have sprouted. If a stalk does not have sprouts, it is discarded.

Furrows are made in the field, and the stalks are laid in them lengthwise. The sprouts grow and a new crop has begun.

The harvesting of both sorghum cane and sugar cane is mechanized today. The making of sorghum syrup has long since left the Panhandle.

207 TEXAS

Chapter 12

Will believed in community involvement. He worked tirelessly and willingly to improve the community where he went to church and his children went to school.

He served as deacon of the church for forty years. He served as trustee on the school board. He served as deputy sheriff. He needed to exercise his authority. A deputy was appointed by the sheriff because it was too far to go from Claude to Wayside. However, he never failed to make the trip at election time, shaking hands, smiling, seeking votes.

One of the men in the community reported to Will that his neighbor was cutting wheat on Sunday. The offender was a friend of Will's, and he thoroughly regretted the step he had to take. He went to the field where his friend was working.

"Good morning, Will."

"Good morning. Nice day."

"Sure is, no wind, nice and dry. The wheat is cutting real good. "

"That is what I came to see you about. You know that you are breaking the law."

"What law?"

"The Sunday Law."

"Never heard of it. Another thing. Nobody tells me what I can or can't do." There was a touch of anger in his voice.

"In 1812, the Legislature passed acts preventing working on Sunday. These acts were brought about because a barber shaved three sailors on Sunday and charged them fifteen cents. I am going to quote to you the law regarding working on Sunday. 'Any person who shall hereafter labor, or compel, force, or oblige his employees, workmen or apprentices to labor on Sunday, or any person who shall hereafter hunt game of any kind whatsoever on Sunday, within one-half mile of any church or private residence, shall be fined not less than ten nor more than fifty dollars.'"

"I don't see how that can apply to me."

"The article I just read was article 299. This is article 300. 'The preceding article shall not apply to household duties, works of necessity or charity, nor to necessary work on farms or plantations in order to prevent the loss of any crop.' Are you about to lose your crop?"

"No, but I have some children to educate."

The friend obeyed the law. A few years later, however, working on Sunday became a custom throughout the nation. The blue law is still in existence, but seldom observed.

Chapter 13

From 1800 to about 1915, all public road work was done by the men whose land bordered the road. They could either work on the road three or four days in the year or pay a road tax of three or four dollars. In some instances, someone would be paid to work in a man's place.

They would use teams, walking plows, and slips to clean out the ditches and build up the low places. These road improvements were crude, but since horse-drawn vehicles were the modes of transportation, they were sufficient.

The road across the Palo Duro was kept passable in this manner. It was a path for those on horseback and a trail for wagons and carts. One day, when the men on the south side were working the road, John McGehee arrived late. He was wearing a broad smile and walking with a slight swagger. "Well, boys, eighteen years from now, I will be Mr. McGehee."

"Oh yeah. How come?"

"I have a new daughter and when she grows up and gets married, her husband will call me Mr. McGehee."

Everyone knew that John and Susie were expecting their first child. They didn't talk about it though. It just wasn't done. Every man there knew that Susie had gone to stay with her mother, who lived about six or seven miles away. They all knew that when labor started, Willis Fisher had gone for Dr. Warner, who lived at Claude, a distance of thirty miles. When he and Dr. Warner got back the next morning, the baby had arrived, screaming her indignation at such harsh treatment. Thereafter, when John and Susie were expecting a baby, they called for Grandma Mayo, the community midwife.

There is a certain select group of people who began life in the Wayside community. Today, they are scattered in all parts of the world.

Some are educated; some are not. Some are rich; some are not. Some have reached influential positions. Some are men; some are women. But they all have one thing in common: they were delivered by Grandma Mayo.

Grandma Mayo was a colorful character. She treated the sick. She helped lay out the dead. She listened to those in trouble. Her treatments were often homemade and self-originated, but many times helpful.

When Curtis McGehee was twelve years of age, he developed a most painful toothache. He had complained for several days. His mother told him to go see Grandma Mayo. Saddling his horse, he rode across the prairie.

"Hello, Curtis. Come in."

Curtis did not reply. His pain-filled eyes just looked at her. "What is the matter? Are you sick?"

Curtis nodded. His swollen jaw should have told her what was wrong. "I have a toothache. Mama told me to come to see you. Maybe you could help me." His eyes were pleading hopefully.

She had him open his mouth as wide as he could. She looked at the irritated tooth. Her rough, work-worn hands gently pressed the swollen area. She clucked in sympathy.

"Son, you go find the jawbone of an animal, hold it to your jaw and run around the house five times. The pain will soon go away."

The prairies were dotted with bleached bones. Curtis soon found the skeleton of a cow, broke off the jawbone, and took it home with him. He placed the bone against his swollen jaw and ran around the house five times. Soon the pain eased and the swelling disappeared.

What was the cure? Who knows?

Chapter 14

December 5, 1917, Will petitioned Happy Masonic Lodge 1008 for the degrees of Masonry.

He was recommended by W. T. Townsend and H. M. Baggarly.

The investigating committee was composed of S. C. Whitman, C. R. Strong, and Josiah Evans.

January 5, 1918, he was initiated and received his first degree.

March 5, 1918, he completed his initiatory work and was passed to the Degree of Fellowcraft.

August 16, 1919, he completed his initiatory work and was raised to Master Mason.

It is believed that the flu epidemic of 1917 and 1918 prevented his completing his work between the second and third degrees at an earlier date.

He was faithful in his attendance. He loved Masonry and placed it second to his church. He lived the farthest distance from Happy and would pick up other members on the way to the meetings.

If the weather prevented going in a car, he went horseback, meeting the other members and riding in a group. One of the members was the instructor. As they rode along the way, they would study their work to prepare for their proficiency.

He visited lodges at Silverton, Tulia, Dimmitt, Roaring Springs, Kansas City, Quitaque, and many other area lodges.

Chapter 15

WILL FIRST BEGAN THINKING ABOUT A ROAD across the Palo Duro when he was helping his father haul cedar posts out of the canyon and selling them for three cents apiece.

He began thinking about it again when he had to go to Claude, the seat of Armstrong County, to pay his taxes, serve on the jury, and [handle] other legal matters. It was a long, arduous trip to cross the canyon horseback or go around it by way of Canyon and Amarillo.

The commissioner for Precinct 2 had always been elected from the north side [of the canyon]. Very little road work was done in the Wayside community. The maintainers could not be brought across the canyon. It was too far to take them around.

In 1928, Will ran for commissioner. He was elected by a comfortable margin. He at once began improving the roads by putting in culverts, building up the low places, putting in drainage ditches. He did not neglect the north side. He began his plan to build a passable road across the Palo Duro. He dared to dream of a paved road in the future.

By 1930, he had a passable road across the canyon from Wayside to Claude. At the meeting of the Commissioners Court, they unanimously voted to call the road Hamblen Drive.

When Will began the task of making the road passable for cars, he followed the original buffalo trail. Today, his equipment would be considered antiquated and obsolete. He used picks and shovels. Slips [were] pulled by a team of horses or mules and handled by one man. Fresnoes were pulled by three or four animals and were operated by two men. One man operated the lever which made the fresno dig in and load with dirt, then dumped it where needed. The wheeler scraper was pulled by a team of four animals and required two men to operate.

The year was 1933. A depression had settled over the land. President Roosevelt declared the nation a disaster area. To provide work

"Canyon Road to Link South and North Plains," Fort Woth Star-Telegram, March 11, 1937. Will Hamblen is shown at lower left.

for those in need, Congress passed the Public Works Administration Act. This act provided salaries for those who engaged in public works such as roads, parks, and forestry. The pay was one dollar per day. Most of the young men, both single and married, in the Wayside area took advantage of the opportunity when Will secured funds for his road through this act.

The men gathered at the Wayside store. Will had a Model A truck. Elvin Wesley had a Model T. Part of the men rode in Elvin's truck while the others went with Will.

The larger implements and equipment were left at the road site, and the animals were left with someone to tend them. All of the small

Modern-day Hamblen Drive, the "Rim to Rim Road," 2012, looking south toward river (photo by Barbara Brannon, Texas Plains Trail Region)

tools were hauled in the trucks. Dynamite was used to blast off the cliffs and move boulders. Will carried the dynamite caps in his lap, while the men sat on the kegs containing the sticks to keep them from rolling around and exploding.

Elvin's truck had no brakes. To keep the truck from getting away from him, he would pull it into the road bank to slow it down, then when it began to gain speed, he would pull it into the bank again.

The men worked with picks and shovels. The slips, fresno, and wheeler scraper were used to move the dirt, smooth the road bed, and fill in around the culverts. As the men cleared the way, the maintainers were able to follow with heavier construction work.

Slowly but surely, the road crept down the canyon wall. The men were not experienced road builders. They were not experienced dynamite men. Loyce Gillham and Will's son, Alfred, volunteered to handle the dynamite. Their respect for the dynamite kept them from getting careless. They were able to complete the project without incident.

When Will saw that his road was going to be a success, he visited with commissioners bordering Armstrong to the south. He tried to in-

Drawing by Richard Jones

terest them in getting the road paved and opening up access roads to the trade running south. The men in Plainview, Lockney, and Floydada were not interested. They could not see any future in the project. When it was too late, they had second thoughts. The trade route to Lubbock, Houston, and Galveston from the north passed them by.

While the crew from the south were working toward the canyon floor, a similar crew was working from the north. The crew found a hill in their path. They argued as to which would be the better route around it. Finally, Mr. Bullier told the men that he would turn his faithful horse loose and let him find his way around the hill. The path that he took would be the direction they would follow. This he did, and to this day that hill is known as Bulliers Hill. The drive around Bulliers Hill is quite different from the one the horse chose. The winding, sweeping drive gives a panoramic view of the Palo Duro that makes the viewer want to drive slower so that it will not pass by too fast.

The crew from the north met the crew from the south at the Prairie Dog [Town] Fork of the Red River. There wasn't much water in it. There never is much water in it. But it was treacherous and thirsty—treacherous with quicksand and thirsty for the unwary.

Will used up all of his county funds. The WPA funds were used up. Will spent many a sleepless night, but he never gave up. Some of the men continued to work for fifty cents per day. There wasn't anything else to do, and fifty cents would buy a little food. Some of the men continued the work, so that the road would be completed. They were also loyal to Will.

With the opening of a passable road, the Palo Duro Canyon was made available to the public. Picnics became a popular excursion. The Palo Duro became the playground of the Panhandle.

Chapter 16

In 1934, the Commissioners Court was faced with a serious problem. County funds were low. They did not know if they would be able to retain the services of the Home Demonstration agent. Funds from each precinct went toward her salary, with the state paying the balance. Will argued against the HD agent. Although he felt that the work of the agent was fine and deserving, he could not leave his road unfinished.

The taxpayers of the precinct became divided. Will had successfully served three terms as commissioner. He was running for a fourth term. The opposition began to function."I tell you, Will will be elected if we don't do something."

"But what can we do?"

"There is only one thing that I know of. We can't change anything on this side. Let's go to the other side. Maybe we can get someone to run against him."

"I don't know who we can get, but maybe some of the fellows across the canyon will know."

The plotters gathered in little groups. Women began going to the club who had never attended before. Monday morning, two of the highly respected, influential men of the community went across the canyon by way of the partially built road and visited with eligible voters. We do not know what arguments they used, but after spending four days of long hours, they were successful in getting an opposing candidate. They electioneered. They talked. Politics had never been so hot and exciting. But Will still retained a majority support in the precinct. The opposing faction could tell that more had to be done if he were to be defeated. The respected and influential men gathered together once more. "Well, what are we going to do?"

W. H. [Will] Hamblen campaign card (Hamblen family collection)

"He is going to be elected, if we don't come up with something."

"You know, I am going to be election judge. These twenty-one-year-old voters get a free vote this year. How many do you suppose there are?"

"Well, let's see. Ethel May, Joyce, Bryce, and isn't Jack twenty-one this year?"

"Yeah, but all of those kids will vote for Will."

"They will, won't they? I'll tell you what I will do. When they come to vote. I won't let them. I will tell them that since they did not pay their poll tax, they can't vote."

"How can you do that? They don't have to pay a poll tax."

"I know it, but if I don't let them vote, it will be too late when they find it out."

The day of the election arrived. The presiding judge and his clerks set up the election procedure. The opposing faction lined up facing Will's supporters. As the voters came in, they were counted. If a voter did not show up, one of the factions was after him, according to which side needed the vote.

Ethel May was excited; it was her first time to vote. She was going to use her prerogative. Proudly, she walked up to the presiding judge.

"Good morning, Ethel May. Did you bring your poll tax receipt?"

"I don't have to have one."

"Yes, you do. Every one must have a poll tax receipt to vote."

"But I get a free vote this year. I am just twenty-one."

"You misunderstand. Even those just twenty-one this year must have a poll tax receipt to vote."

Ethel May did not think that she had misunderstood. Disappointed, she turned away. This procedure went on all day. When the votes were counted, Will had lost by two votes.

There was great rejoicing in the camp of the opposition. They went back to their respective homes and took up their respective business enterprises, satisfied with a job well done. Their satisfaction was short-lived.

Will could not hire a member of his own family to work on the road, but the new commissioner could. He immediately hired Will's son and son-in-law to operate the maintainers used in the road construction. There were screams of anguish. The boys continued to work. Mr. Scroggins continued to use his own judgment in the fulfillment of his obligation, seemingly oblivious to the wishes of his electors.

Mr. Scroggins served as commissioner for two years. He announced for reelection. Will entered the race again. The north side of the precinct had second thoughts about listening to the opposition. The young people, who had been denied the right to vote, did not forget. Will began a career on the Armstrong County Commissioners Court that continued for eighteen years.

Chapter 17

The years from the time Will and Ada established their home on a section of land in Armstrong County were a continual changing scene. They were scenes of depression and prosperity; scenes of drought and lush, green pastures. A scene that spanned three wars.

Will was a stockman and trader. He raised cattle, horses, and mules. World War I developed a market for mules. Will bought and traded for the war market. The market was good for horses, too, but more so for mules.

The armed forces were not mechanized in World War I. Animals were used to move supplies. The troops walked—and walked—and walked. Mules were used on the front, because they would walk over dead bodies. Horses would not, and there was no time to fool around with squeamish animals.

Before local cattle markets were established, Will shipped carloads of cattle to the markets in Kansas City. He would buy up enough cattle to combine with his own to make several carloads. When he first began to ship cattle, the Panhandle of Texas was a vast expanse of prairie. Riding in the caboose, Will watched daylight fade into night. He watched a velvet blanket of darkness hover, then settle over the land. As the long cattle train snaked its way across the prairie, there were miles that no light could be seen.

As the years passed, oil fields opened up, towns grew; the view from the caboose changed. The velvet blanket was almost obscured by the bright lights that covered the countryside.

Will witnessed the gradual change of the Great Plains from a great cattle country to a farming country, where people gambled life and labor on the production of wheat. A land of few trails to paved highways. A land where his ambition changed from breaking horses to building a road.

Horses and mule teams used on the Rolling Plains

In 1910, Will built a new house for his family. The contractor was Manny Howard. The house was frame construction, sealed inside with shiplap and siding on the outside. The downstairs section contained five rooms. A wide hall and staircase led to two rooms upstairs. There was no running water in the house, and the john was an ordinary outdoor john. About 1940, the federal government allocated funds and

Hamblen family home, Wayside, Armstrong County, circa 1940s (Hamblen family collection)

W. H. (Will) Hamblen and family, circa 1934 (Hamblen family collection)

hired men to go to the farms and build pit johns. A pit about six feet deep was dug in a place not more than fifty feet from the dwelling (federal decision), then the little house with air vents on the side was placed over it.

Will and Ada lived in this house for fifty years. Fourteen children were born to this union, of which nine are still living. The house is still on the original homestead and [has been] used as a residence of a Hamblen since its erection. Put together with seasoned lumber and lots of nails, it will probably stand for another sixty-one years.[4]

Will saw farm operations change through technology from a two-horse walking plow to a six-team riding plow, to steam-operated engines, to powerful gasoline-, then butane-burning motors.

He saw harvest machines develop from the one-row binder to a broadcast, to the header and barge, to the tractor-drawn combine to the present day air-conditioned, enclosed, self-propelled combine. The belt-driven threshing machine was quite an innovation but gradually gave way to the combine.

He saw the Model T improved upon by the Model A, then by modern automobiles of today.

Will was modern in his thinking. With each new development, he updated his farming methods. Gradually his section of grassland became a section of farm land. He bought and leased other farm and pasture land.

The Depression of the thirties hurt Will, just as it did everyone. Wheat dropped to fifteen cents per bushel. There was no market for livestock. The horse and mule market was nonexistent. He disposed of most of his stock for whatever he could get for it. He always kept a few horses. He continued to trade in cattle. But he hung on. His banker never gave up on him. Many farmers had to give up their holdings and move away. This was the beginning of the decline in population in the community.

On December 7, 1941, the Japanese bombed Pearl Harbor. President Roosevelt declared war against Japan, and World War II was born. Prices for farm commodities rose to an all-time high. Will recovered

---

4. Sadly, after the original homestead was sold in 1987–88, the home was bulldozed in 2010.

from the Depression. When Uncle Sam asked for volunteers, Will's youngest son, Oleff, answered the call.

In 1950, the United Nations decided that South Korea needed protection from communist North Korea. American troops were deployed to the 38th parallel as a police force. Two of Will's grandsons, Alfred Beryl and William Henry Hamblen, carried on the American tradition of loyalty to their country.

Chapter 18

When Will settled his family on his land near Wayside, he began the battle of supporting his growing family. He also began a battle with the elements of nature. The winters [seemed] more harsh and severe than they are today. There were no weathermen with radar equipment to inform him of approaching storms.

During the winter of 1914, a blizzard blew in and heavy snow fell for three days and nights. Will cared for the stock inside pens near the house. Those out on the range had to take care of themselves.

When the storm abated and Will and his son could get their horses out of the stable, they went looking for cattle. Will had three huge stacks of wheat straw left from threshing on the farm. He checked these haystacks first.

During the fall before the storm struck, the cattle had eaten into the haystacks, forming caves. Will and his son Alfred found the haystacks covered with snow, obscuring the caves. They felt sure that the cattle had taken refuge in the caves. Alfred noticed little puffs of smoke coming from a small hole in the snow. It was the breath of the cattle condensing as it hit the frosty air. Will left the cattle in their shelter where they had plenty to eat and could quench their thirst with snow.

June 23, 1920, was a cloudy day, cool and threatening rain. Will and Alfred had been attending to stock in pastures away from home. Will was in a buggy, carrying fence repair material and other equipment. In the afternoon, when they had finished their work, they started for home. Will proceeded on home but sent Alfred to another pasture to check some gates.

A dark cloud had built up in the north. It was moving rapidly, rolling, seething, and white caps outlined its peaks. The wind had been blowing out of the west all day. In an instant, the wind changed and came out of the cloud, icy cold. Will had already arrived at home, but

Alfred was still on the way. He knew the cloud was dangerous and began racing his horse for shelter. Without warning, baseball-sized hail began to fall at the same time as a drenching rain.

Alfred leaped from his horse and stood as close to his shoulders as he could get, pulling the saddle stirrups over his head for protection. He had never liked this horse and considered him to be a rather poor specimen. He changed his mind, for the horse lowered his head and took the brunt of the storm. providing protection which Alfred felt sure saved his life.

Cattle and horses were killed by the hail. Some were so badly bruised that they died later. Trees were cut to shreds. The north side of fence posts were stripped bare of bark. All birds and small wild animals in its path were killed. The rain was so heavy, about four inches in forty-five minutes, that the brooks and fields were awash. Any small animal that survived the hail drowned.

Wiatt Heisler was in a field working six head of mules to a breaking plow. When he saw the cloud, he immediately started for home. The storm struck while he was about one-half mile from the house. His team panicked, broke away, and rushed to the barn. Wiatt lost his hat, trying to hold onto his team. He had nothing to protect his head from the pounding hail except his Levi's jacket. He folded his arms over his head and tried to keep from drowning with his jacket. A short distance from shelter seemed like miles in pounding hail and fear for one's life.

The hail was of such volume that the running water washed it into drifts. Dave Hamblen, Will's brother, hitched a team to a wagon and went to the small brook running near his home. Using a scoop shovel, he filled his wagon with ice. He piled it on the north side of a windbreak and covered it with cane or milo bundles. On July 4, he made ice cream with this ice.

The storm was ten miles wide. It began north of Amarillo and extended as far south as Quitaque. No one within the path of its devastation has forgotten this storm.

207
TEXAS

Chapter 19

Ada stood out in the yard looking at the rising sun. The ball of gold was clear and bright. Her eyes followed the blue sky to the west. The dark horizon faded to sunlight as her glance swept upward. The anxious look left her face as she returned to the house. "Girls, let's get the washing started. It is going to be a nice day."

Preparations began for getting the family wash on the line. Ada's first laundry equipment consisted of a black wash pot, zinc tubs, and a brass wash board. She made her soap out of cracklings and lye. By 1933, Ada had a wringer-type Maytag washing machine. She still had to heat the water in a black iron pot.

Since Ada's family was large, even with a washing machine it took several hours to do the laundry. By ten o'clock, little gusts of wind could be seen and felt. It could be seen because it picked up little puffs of sand. Ada looked to the west again. The horizon was not clear and blue. A haze was rising into the sky. The wind grew stronger. She looked across the way to neighboring fields. The wind was picking up the soil as it moved across the land. The girls hurried with the laundry. As they hung the clothes on the line, the wind dried them quickly. As fast as they dried, they were brought into the house and others hung out.

By noon, the sun was a dim ball of fire through the dirt. The sand made a good filter. One could look directly into the sun and suffer no damage. About three o'clock, the sky was black. The dirt movement began in Colorado, crossed the shallow-tilled wheatfields of New Mexico, crossed the Texas and Oklahoma borders. Rolling, boiling, and foaming it rolled. Ada and the girls closed all the windows, placing wet newspapers under the window sashes.

A black dirt storm was a fascinating thing to watch. The wind current could be followed by the movement of dirt. Because of the weight of dirt, the cloud moved slowly. When it hit the house, there was to-

Dust storm during the 1930s

tal darkness for several minutes. The air was stifling. Burning lamps flickered. The house filled with a fine silt. As the dirt cloud moved on, the sky lightened but the sun did not shine through. At the end of the day, the wind would subside; the dust began to settle and the air clear. However, on several occasions, the wind and dirt would blow for three or four days without ceasing.

Those were the Dust Bowl days. Those were the days that tried men's souls. Will watched the soil blow away to the hardpan. The only thing that seemed to thrive on drought conditions was the Russian thistle. The tiny, thin blade came up early in the spring. They grew into round, green balls of many sizes. In early fall, the thistle dried into a hard, round ball, broke loose from its shallow roots, and started rolling with the wind. The weed was covered with hard, prickly spikes. These spikes were seed pods, and as the weed rolled, it sowed the seed for the next year.

There was beauty in a field of rolling thistles. The smaller thistles seemed to be playing tag as they touched, then raced away. The little ones seemed to stumble and fall, then get up and hurriedly try to catch up. They reminded [one] of antelope, jumping, leaping, and whirling as they frolicked.

Following behind were the big, lumbering thistles. Several feet in diameter, they rolled more slowly. As the wind gusted, they picked up speed. Walking over fences, piling up in the barrow ditches. Filling in low places. Elephants marching.

Many of the farmers found that the thistle had one good quality. Ground and mixed with syrup, they made good cow feed. Cacti also made good cow feed if the thorns were knocked off and they were chopped into bite-size pieces.

And then the rains came.

Chapter 20

THE PIONEER SETTLERS IN THE WAYSIDE COMMUNITY worked hard all week and went to church on Sunday. At church, they met and visited with all of their friends and neighbors. They introduced themselves to visitors, making them feel welcome. The boys met their girls. The girls looked for a fellow. There wasn't anything else to do. If there was anyone in the community who did not go to church, he was looked upon with disfavor.

There were dances for those who danced. The dances were held in the home. All of the furniture would be moved out of the room. Benches made of boards placed on nail kegs or chairs, or anything that would hold them, were placed around the walls, leaving the center of the room for dancing. The music was a fiddle accompanied by a guitar. Usually, only two musicians performed. Sometimes a banjo would be added. Sometimes they were paid, but more often they played because they loved to play.

The waltz, two-step, foxtrot and turkey trot were some of the dance steps. Occasionally, there would be a square dance. Folk dances were popular. The schottische, Put-Your-Little-Foot (sometimes called New Shoes), Glowworm, Blackhawk Waltz, Rye Waltz, Range Rider polka, all were popular folk dances. The girls were good dancers. Most of the boys were good dancers. Some of the cowboys made up their own steps and danced the same for every dance regardless of the tempo of the music. They had more fun than anyone.

Game parties were held for those who did not dance. Some of the games played by the teenagers and young adults were Spin the Bottle, Snap, Last Couple Out, Musical Chairs, and Post Office.

If a family owned a piano, all the young people in the community would gather at the home and sing. Quite often the older people joined in. When Will gave up a pair of mules for an upright grand piano, his family was most surprised. They would never have thought it of him. Will and Ada's home was always open to visitors and to the young people. They had parties and singings, but they did not dance. When the word was received that a party was going to be held at a home where dancing was allowed, mothers quizzed their children at great length, to be sure that it was in fact a party and not a dance.

Another source of entertainment was fruit suppers. The boys would take a can of fruit; the girls would take a cake. After playing games for two or three hours, the fruit and cake would be served for refreshments. Fruit suppers were held in the fall and winter and ice cream suppers in the summer.

Singing schools were held in the summer. Transient singing teachers would book a school to be held in the school or church house. They taught many boys and girls to read music. The instructors would charge so much per person, and the school usually lasted two weeks with a great finale at the end to show what the students had learned.

The teachers taught sight reading, round and square notes, keys, and the different singing voices, and strangely enough, some good singers developed from these schools. The schools lasted ten days. The teachers were always men.

Those were the days of the past, dimmed with the passing of time.

Chapter 21

METHODISM CAME TO THE COMMUNITY with the Fishers, Bradfords and McGehees. The McSpaddens were Presbyterian. The entire settlement worshiped in the one-room school house for several years. Occasionally, some of the people went to Salem for church services. They would spend the day with dinner on the ground.

Each family carried baskets of food. Tables were set up on the church or schoolhouse grounds and the food [was] spread on them. The tables were boards placed on sawhorses or other support. The ladies brought tablecloths and covered the boards. It was a day of visiting and socializing.

Every one went to church. All denominations worshiped together. In the absence of a minister, John Fisher and J. H. Bradford conducted services.

Below: Wayside church and school building, drawing by Richard Jones

Above: Wayside Community Church, circa 1971

In 1908, Arthur Coleman, an ordained minister, led in the organization of the Beulah Baptist Church. Will and Ada had been raised in Christian homes, but neither had a church affiliation. They joined the Beulah Baptist Church as charter members. Clara McClain also joined as a charter member. She is the only living member today.

In 1909, a Methodist minister, Mr. Fort, who preached at both Wayside and Vigo Park, began the project of building a church. John and Susie McGehee gave the land for both a Methodist and a Baptist church. Susie was a Baptist and John a Methodist. He did not want to be partial. The site of the Methodist location was right across the road from the cemetery. The site of the Baptist location was on forty acres deeded to the community for development.

The leaders in the denominations gathered together and decided that there were not enough of either denomination to have separate churches. They decided to build a community church. Don Adams, a Baptist, and David McGehee, a Methodist, solicited funds for the building.

After securing enough money to buy the lumber, Mannie and Aubrey Howard and Tom Green were hired as carpenters. Men of the community donated their time as they could.

In the spring of 1910, the first services were held in the new church. It was a great day and every one attended. Arthur Coleman was the first Baptist pastor and Mr. Fort was the Methodist.

On October 26, 1910, Clara McClain and Curtis McGehee were united in marriage in the new church, the first wedding performed there. The officiating minister was Arthur Coleman, Clara's brother-in-law. Curtis had built a new house for his bride. They held the reception in their new home. Every man, woman, and child went to the wedding. Every man, woman, and child went to the reception.

Sunday morning, November 19, 1933, was bright and clear. Every one had gone to church. One family was late. When they arrived in sight of the church, they were horrified to see flames breaking through the roof. Rushing to the church, the woman jumped from the car and dashed into the building. "The church is on fire!"

No one paid any attention to her.

"I tell you the church is on fire!"

This time they listened. Hurriedly, they moved from the church, carrying what they could with them. Just before the last person left the building, the ceiling began to fall in.

The building was heated with a coal stove, and the fire had caught around the vent in the roof.

Church services were held in the schoolhouse until a new building could be erected. Community church services are conducted to the present in this building.

In 1927, the name of the Baptist church was changed from Beulah Baptist to Wayside Baptist Church.

207
TEXAS

Chapter 22

Nancy Alverson was born in Mississippi, November 7, 1850. Her father owned slaves, one of whom was her beloved "Negro Aimy." Nancy could remember Negro Aimy taking her on her lap, resting her head on her soft bosom, gently rocking and softly crooning. Childish cares vanished and hurts healed quickly. In 1859, her father moved to Tarrant County. We do not know what became of Negro Aimy and the other slaves.

The long trek was made in a covered wagon drawn by slow, plodding oxen. Her father walked beside the wagon, guiding them with a twenty-foot leather bullwhip. The heavy, wooden yoke around the necks of the oxen helped prevent any attempt at breaking loose.

Nancy remembered, vividly, her journey through Arkansas. So many of the people became sick of fever. Many did not reach their destination in Texas. Forever after, Nancy felt a strong dislike for Arkansas.

When the Civil War broke out, Nancy was eleven years old. She remembered watching the men walking away from home as they left to join the army. She was a staunch supporter of the Confederacy and of Robert E. Lee.

Fruit was scarce in the new country. Wild plums grew on the small creeks near Nancy's home. She helped pick the plums which were used to make jelly and plum butter, and canned to be used in pies. One day when Nancy was on the creek with other children, the Indians seized a six-year-old boy, carrying him into captivity. He returned to his parents' home twelve years later, as wild and uncivilized as his captors. He was never able to adjust to civilized life. After running away several times, he finally left and did not return.

Nancy was sixteen years old when Napoleon Bonaparte Thornton came riding up to her father's farm. He had a bedroll strapped to the back of his saddle and a guitar hung from his shoulder. Travelers were always welcome at the Alverson home. Nat Thornton was invited to spend the night. He entertained the family by playing his guitar and singing. Nancy thought one of his songs was more beautiful than any of the others. "Mr. Thornton, what is the name of that song?"

"'Red River Valley.'"

As long as she lived, "Red River Valley" was Nancy's favorite song.

Mr. Alverson offered Nat a job hauling freight from Fort Worth. Nat accepted the offer and worked for Mr. Alverson on separate occasions for two years.

Romance developed between Nancy and Nat. On August 19, 1869, they were married. They made their home in Missouri for several years, then moved to Newark in Erath County. Nat continued to work for Mr. Alverson for a time, then began his own business operations.

Nat made infrequent, mysterious trips. At times, he would be gone for a few days; at times, he would be gone for several weeks. Nancy's only son was fourteen years old when his father left for the last time. If Nancy ever heard from him or had news about him, she never mentioned it. Her oldest daughter, Sue, had married Tom Bussell. Their home was near Nancy's.

When Nat left for the last time, he gave his son-in-law, Tom Bussell, a money belt, which contained $57,000.00 and told him to take care of Nancy. Two years after Nat left, Nancy moved her family to Swisher County, locating in the area where Kress is. Nancy bought four sections of land. Tom and Sue filed on a section. Both families lived in dugouts. Nancy's other two daughters married. One of them, Emma Lou, married Robert Alan Hoover. John Alan Hoover of Canyon is a great-grandson of Nancy Alverson Thornton.

John Alan relates this story about his grandmother's marriage. Robert Alan was working on a ranch. On the day of his marriage, he was riding to the home of his fiancée, Emma Lou. He had traded his horse for another, paying some cash difference. On the way, some riders overtook him and accused him of stealing the horse. He denied the charges, but in those days, a horse thief was first hanged, then asked if he were guilty. Just before the rope tightened around his neck, some riders came in and declared that he was indeed innocent of stealing the horse. Nancy's daughter and Robert Alan were married and established their home in West Texas.

An interview with Jessie Hill of Portales, a granddaughter of Nancy Thornton, relates the hardships endured by the families while living in Swisher County. They had to haul water in barrels. They had no meat. They had no vegetables or fruit. At one time, Jessie's mother saved the eggs until she had enough for the family to have eggs for breakfast. The great day arrived. The mother started breaking the eggs, and each one of them was blood-red. The chickens had no grain to eat and had been feeding on grasshoppers. Jessie said that she could remember crying in her disappointment and hunger.

On another occasion, Jessie's father killed a stray steer. It had been so long since they had meat to eat. He dressed out the carcass and told Jessie to take some of the meat to her grandmother. Even though Jessie was quite small, she clearly remembers carrying the meat to her grandmother's house, followed by wolves, which had been attracted by the smell of fresh meat.

In 1903 or 1905, Nancy sold her land in Swisher County and bought a tract of land near Taiban, New Mexico. She stocked the land with horses and cattle. She purchased a two-room house for twenty-five dollars. She always paid cash in her transactions.

This was the time of the comancheros. They raided the ranches, driving off the horses and cattle. Nancy lost practically everything that she had gained.

Nancy moved again. She sold her land at Taiban and purchased a tract near Bula in Crosby County.[5] She lived at this location until 1910, then moved to Parmer County, near Friona. She purchased several sections of land, paying cash. Nancy Thornton had no visible signs of support, yet she always had plenty of money.

Over the years, Nancy became known as Grandmother Thornton. She lived on her ranch alone until she was ninety. She rode horseback, having a favorite mount. He was old and fat. He was so broad across the back, a saddle would hardly stay on. He always carried his rider as if he

---

5. While the author says that Bula was in Crosby County, standard sources show this town, an unincorporated community, situated in Bailey County.

knew she was something special, and he must take care of her. When he died, Grandmother Thornton never rode again. She gave several excuses, but everyone knew that it was because her beloved horse would not be carrying her.

When Grandmother Thornton was 101, she fell and broke her arm and her hip. The arm healed, but the hip did not. She moved to Friona, making her home with a granddaughter, spending the balance of her days in a wheelchair.

Nancy's granddaughter kept her grandmother like a museum piece. Nancy was small of physique. Her white hair was immaculate. She had a number of lovely shawls. Each day, when she was ready for visitors, she had on a shawl and a corsage. Her face was powdered with rice powder. She received visitors from three to five p.m. She died at the age of 107, slipping quietly and easily into the unknown while in her sleep.

Where did Nat get the $57,000.00 that he gave to his son in-law Tom Bussell?

Rube Burris was the most famed outlaw in Texas history. He robbed banks, but his specialty was train robberies. Rube was one of the most notorious of the Jesse James gang.

Nat was his partner.

Chapter 23

IN 1902, WHILE WILL AND ADA WERE STILL LIVING in the Palo Duro, his father, S. P. Hamblen, sold his land on the rim of the canyon and filed on a tract in the Palo Duro. Cowboys for the JA Ranch filed on tracts of land, then sold them to the JA owner. Each cowboy was allowed, by law, to file on only one tract of land. Sterling checked the land records and found that one of the men had filed on more than one tract. He filed on one of the same tracts and moved his family into the canyon.

Their first shelter was made of poles stuck into the side of a sand bank and covered with cloth, then covered with brush and dirt. This served until a dugout was built.

Word got back to the JA headquarters that some squatters were on

Dugout house, drawing by William Clay, '67

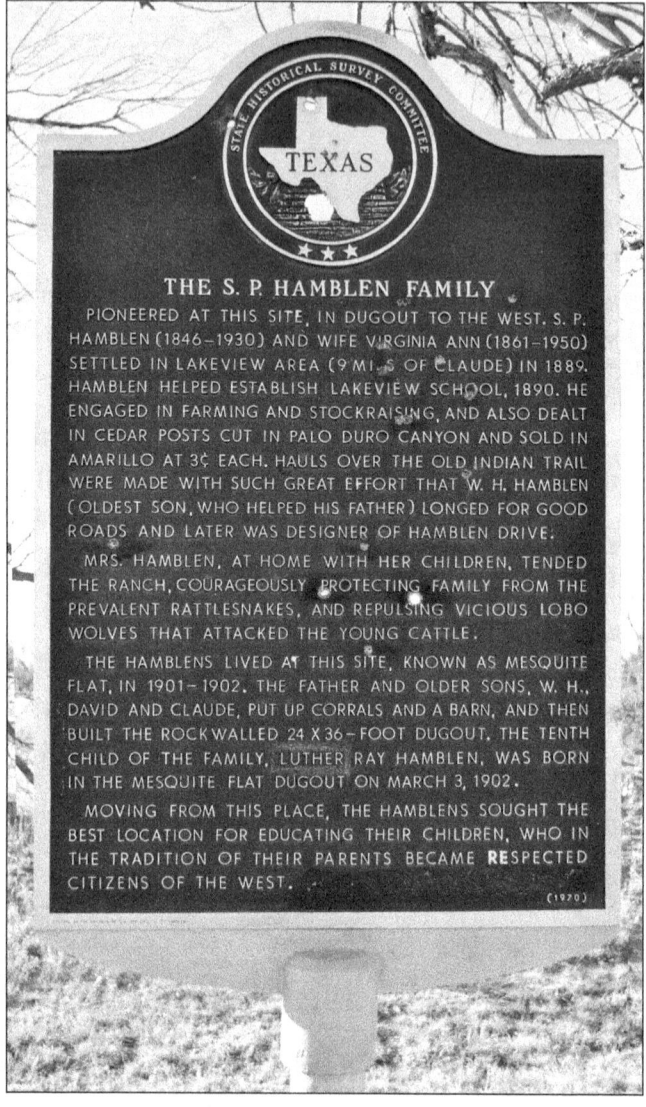

S. P. Hamblen Family historical marker on site of corrals and barn, 2012 (photo by Barbara Brannon, Texas Plains Trail Region)

ranch property. Some of the boys rode out to see about it. They found Sterling and his family settled and told them they would have to move. Sterling refused. He had filed on his claim and had a legal right to stay there. The men rode off.

A few weeks later, the men returned. They came early in the morning, just at break of day. Sterling went into the yard to meet them. He saw that they were wearing guns. He knew that if he tried to stand his ground, someone could get hurt, maybe some member of his family, so he gave up his claim and moved back to the Henry Dye place, where he farmed on shares and wages.

The site of the old dugout still remains, the rock walls a reminder of the toil and physical effort that went into their building. On July 24, 1970, a historical marker was erected at the site of the dugout, a memorial to the dominant spirit of a Panhandle pioneer.

Citation on historical marker:

> S. P. Hamblen family pioneered at this site, in dugout to the west. S. P. Hamblen (1846–1930) and wife Virginia Ann (1861–1950) settled in Lakeview area (9 mi. S. of Claude) in 1889. Hamblen helped establish Lakeview School, 1890. He engaged in farming and stock raising and also dealt in cedar posts cut in Palo Duro Canyon and sold in Amarillo at 3 cents each. Hauls over the old Indian trail were made with such great effort that W. H. Hamblen (oldest son, who helped his father) longed for good roads and later was designer of Hamblen Drive. Mrs. Hamblen, at home with her children, tended the ranch, courageously protecting family from the prevalent rattlesnakes, and repulsing vicious lobo wolves that attacked the young cattle. The Hamblens lived at this site, known as Mesquite Flat, in 1901–1902. The father and older sons, W. H., David and Claude, put up corrals and a barn, and then built the rockwalled 24 x 36-foot dugout. The tenth child of the family, Luther Ray Hamblen, was born in the Mesquite Flat dugout on March 3, 1902. Moving from this place, the Hamblens sought the best location for educating their children, who in the tradition of their parents became respected citizens of the west.

Hamblen Drive, early photos

Chapter 24

After Hamblen Drive had been open to the public for several years, the federal government requested that a traffic survey be made. After the survey, the government stated that no more funds could be spent on the road. This was a real blow to both Claude and Wayside. Everyone knew that if there were not funds to keep the road in repair, it would become impassable. The river needed to be watched because it was constantly changing channels. Every time there was a rise, the channel changed. There were rock slides and mud slides. The quicksand was dangerous to those unaware.

Will and the commissioners discussed the problem, seeking for a way to keep the road. Will and Dr. Warner of Claude went to Austin and met with the [Texas] Highway Commission, requesting that a farm-to-market road be built. They pleaded their cause earnestly and fervently. The commission listened with courtesy and attention. They committed nothing. Later, three delegates including Will and Charlie Stewart of Claude met with the commission, again pleading their cause. Again the commission listened politely. Again they were noncommittal. The men were almost discouraged. Houston and Galveston were there asking for millions, and Will and his men were only asking for hundreds of thousands. They did not give up.

The Armstrong County commissioners, businessmen, and county judge visited Pampa, Borger, and Phillips, asking for their cooperation in seeking a paved road that would connect the trade markets of the North and South Plains. They went to Lubbock asking for support.

More trips to Austin with additional support seemed to meet with the same result. Mr. Lott, district highway engineer, was stationed in Amarillo. He turned a cold shoulder toward the building of an FM across the Palo Duro. Chili Smith was his assistant. It is thought that

Top: Hamblen Drive, aerial photo (Hamblen family collection). Bottom: Hamblen Drive, showing bridge across Prairie Dog Town Fork of the Red River (Amarillo Globe-News photo, 1968)

these men probably knew more about the thinking of the Highway Commission than they seemed to.

Feeling that they had done their best and that there was nothing more. that they could do, they let the matter ride, and for several years no work was done on the road. As they knew would happen, the road became almost impassable for cars.

But the State Highway Commission had not forgotten the proposed road. They had been aware of the need even before Will and his delegation met with them. At that time there were no funds to work with. There was another reason why they were aware of the need for a road.

When the United States became involved in World War II, the federal government became concerned with national defense. Traffic engineers were sent to all of the large cities in the nation to survey evacuation routes in case of an air raid from the enemy. These routes would also be used for the movement of troops and troop supplies. Upon checking the city of Amarillo, they found that there were plenty of routes running east and west but only one running north and south.

About 1946 or '47, the state decided to move. Funds were available for the road. Mr. Lott was not enthusiastic, but the engineer in Lubbock was helping in every way that he could. The state asked the Armstrong County commissioners to secure the right-of-way for the road. They had no money. Will went to his friend John McGehee and asked him to loan the county some money. John told him that he did not have it right then but to give him two or three days. John loaned the county about $6,000.00 at 6 per cent. After securing the right-of-way, Mr. Bailey, bridge engineer with the State Highway Commission,[6] was sent to Claude to inspect and select a route for the road. He picked up Mr. Lott and Chili Smith in Amarillo, then Charlie Stewart at Claude.

They drove across the canyon seeking the best possible route. They followed Will's road from the north to Tobe Smith Flat, then east of the old trail following the backbone to the south side. This route missed Wayside by five miles.

Will and John McGehee went to Claude in a pickup and asked Charlie Stewart to ride with them up the river. They were sure that they could find a way out that would put the road through Wayside. They rode up and down the river, but even John and Will could see that the engineer was right. The State also argued that to go any other route would necessitate the building of two bridges across the river instead of one. John McGehee was more disappointed that anyone at the route chosen. He wanted so badly for the road to go through Wayside.

207
TEXAS

---

6. The author is likely referring, here, to the Texas Highway Department, the state agency at the time, rather than the commission.

Chapter 25

AFTER THE WORK BEGAN, IT WENT RATHER QUICKLY. The road equipment was a far cry from the slips, two-wheelers, and dynamite Will used. In a few months the road was completed and in 1954 opened to traffic. The huge modern concrete bridge, 975 feet long, spans the Prairie Dog, taking away the horror and fear of the quicksand. The total amount of dirt and rock moved in grading and excavating with mammoth dirt-moving equipment amounted to 565,800 cubic yards.

It was rather interesting to get the reaction of several of the workers. One was asked, "What are you doing?" His reply was, "I am working for $1.10 an hour." Another was asked the same question, and his reply was, "I am mixing concrete." A third man was asked the same question, and his reply was, "I am helping to build a road."

When Marshall Formby of Plainview was appointed to the Highway Commission, the Texas Panhandle felt that for the first time they had representation in Austin. He knew Farm-to-Market 284. When the Post-to-Borger Highway Association began working for a state highway through the Palo Duro, he knew the area they were talking about. From Post the road would go south through San Angelo into Del Rio. It would go north from Borger to Kansas, Nebraska, and to the Canadian border. Farm-to-Market 284 had a grade of 8 percent, some of it running as high as 9 percent. The state highway required a grade of not more than 6-1/2 percent. The statement has been made that in our time the high grade will be cut down.

In 1958, the state designated that FM 284 be State Highway 207. At 10:00 a.m. May 28, 1958, the county judge, Richard Morris, presided at the ribbon cutting which took place on the north side. Marshall Formby was the honored guest and represented the state Highway Department. When the time came to cut the ribbon, John McGehee held the scissors. The entourage rode across the Palo Duro to the south side and returned.

The road is still called Hamblen Scenic Drive, and markers designating it as such are in the process of being erected. Forty years of hard work, discouragement, struggle, and determination yielded an honor few men receive.

The drive is spectacular in color and scenery. The long, white ribbon of concrete winds in long, sloping curves, dips into valleys, then stretches across flat plains. The red clay walls, sliced through the hills, are embedded with white gypsum. The soft ruffle of the Spanish Skirts outlines the canyon rim. The deepest cut believed in any road in Texas is in the Palo Duro; the steep walls of red rock are underlain by red clay of the same color.

The only rest area is located on top of a high pinnacle that overlooks the canyon to the north. Steep cliffs descend to the floor of the canyon. A tight steel fence follows the pinnacle rim. On each side of the paved area are two shaded picnic tables. In the center is a marker which reads:

Hamblen Drive

Named for Will H. Hamblen (1878–1952), who in 1890's pioneered a crude road (about 6 mi. N) into Palo Duro Canyon along old Indian trails. This cut 120 miles off settlers' trips to court house in Claude, but was steep and dangerous. Hamblen and his wife, Ada (1883–1955) ranched near Wayside after 1905. He worked unceasingly to get a passable road through Palo Duro. Elected county commissioner in 1928, he at last had a graded road built. By decision of the commissioners' court, road was dedicated in 1930 as Hamblen Drive. With its paving in 1954, a dream of a lifetime was realized.

Chapter 26

Thursday morning, November 24, 1952, Will stepped out his front door and walked out onto the sidewalk. He surveyed the peaceful  scene around him. He looked at the rising sun. He felt the cool, crisp air. There was nothing about this scene to indicate that this would be the last time that he would walk out his front door. It would be the last time that he would see the sun rising.

He turned and walked to the post office. In his mail was a notice regarding an automobile accident that he had recently been involved in. Will started across the street to the office of his insurance carrier.

The street was covered with snow and ice. Will stepped onto a slick strip of ice and fell backwards, striking his head against the sharp, jagged chunks.

He was placed in the hospital. The attending physician told his family that if he lived eight days, he would be all right. His skull was fractured, and it was feared there was brain damage. Eight days later, December 2, 1952, the trail Will had been following for seventy-six years reached the other side.

Will Hamblen, late in life, driving mule team (Hamblen family collection)

Texas historical marker for Hamblen Drive, roadside park, south side of Palo Duro Canyon along Texas Highway 207, spring 2013 (photo by Barbara Brannon, Texas Plains Trail Region)

Acknowledgments

The editors of this volume wish to thank Lynn Canafax, granddaughter of Eutha Hamblen, for providing three original drawings. Additional photographs were provided by various members of the Hamblen family. Elizabeth Mitchell scanned and checked the text and images from the first edition, in preparation for this newly typeset edition, during her 2013 internship with the Texas Plains Trail Region at West Texas A&M University. Barbara Brannon, executive director of the Texas Plains Trail Region, handled copyediting, page layout, and cover design of the new edition.

For Further Reading

Readers may learn more about the communities mentioned in this book, about Wayside and Armstrong County, and about the Hamblen family in other standard sources:

Armstrong County Historical Association, *A Collection of Memories: A History of Armstrong County, 1876–1965* (Hereford, Texas: Pioneer, 1965).
Awbrey, Betty Dooley, and Stuart Awbrey, eds., with The Texas Historical Commission, *Why Stop?: A Guide to Texas Roadside Historical Markers* (Dallas: Taylor Trade Publishing, 2013), p 101.
Texas State Historical Association, Handbook of Texas Online, www.tshaonline.org/handbook/online, s.v. Hamblen, William Henry; Wayside, TX (Armstrong County).

About the Texas Plains Trail Region and Its Imprint

The Texas Plains Trail Region, established in 2003 as a nonprofit organization in the state of Texas, is an award-winning heritage tourism initiative of the Texas Historical Commission representing 52 counties of the Texas Plains and Panhandle. Through promotion, preservation, and education, the Texas Plains Trail Region assists in the development of its unique cultural, heritage, and natural resources for communities and their visitors.

As an extension of its educational mission, the Texas Plains Trail Region founded Texas Plains Trail Books in 2013, during its tenth-anniversary year, to preserve and distribute works of historical and cultural significance in print and digital formats.

To learn more about the region, plan your travel adventure, or participate in our work, visit **www.TexasPlainsTrail.com.**

Index

Numbers in italics denote illustrations.

Abilene, Kansas, 32
Adair, Cornelia, 23
Adams, Don, 95
Alverson (Thornton), Nancy, 97–100
Alverson, Mr., 98
Amarillo, Texas, 11, 39, 41, 43, 64, 74, 88, 103, 105, 107
Armstrong County Commission, 11, 74, 79, 81, 107, 109
Armstrong County, 9, 11, 21, 23, 74, 82
Austin, capital of Texas, 105

Baggarly, H. M., 73
Bailey, Mr., 107
Baker Mercantile, 42–45
Baker, Alice, 41, 43–44
Baker, Francis, 41, 42, 43
Baker, James Artemas, 41–45
Ballard, Mr., 43
Battle of Pease River, 29
Bell, Mitch, 47, 51
Beulah Baptist Church (Wayside Baptist Church), 95, 96
Beulah community and school, 37, 39
Beverly store, 39
Big Blue River, 47, 55
Block pasture, 64
blue laws, 69–70
Blue-Back Speller, 21
Borger, Hutchinson County, 105, 108
Bradford family, 36, 94
Bradford, Cassie, 39

Bradford, J. H., 94
Bradford, Mr., 39, 65
Bradford, Mrs., 38
Bradshaw, Bertie, 38
Bryce, 80
buffalo trails, 35, 36, 74
Bula, Bailey County, 99
Bullier, Mr., 77
Bulliers Hill, 77
Burris, Rube, 100
Bussell, Sue Thornton, 98
Bussell, Tom, 98, 100

Camp Pleasant, 46
Canadian River, 32–34, 37, 55
Canyon Senior Citizens, 10
Canyon, Randall County, 11, 74
Carey, J. C., 25–26, 31
cattle ranching and selling, 46–52; *50*; 82, 85, 87–88, 91
Chisholm Trail, 32
Christian, Jim, 60–61
chuck wagon, 47–48, *50*
churches, 62–63, 94–96, *94, 95*
Civil War, 19, 97
Clarendon, Donley County, 49
Claude, Armstrong County, 9, 11, 17, 21, 24, 35, 39, 64, 71, 74, 105, 109
Coleman, Arthur, 95–96
Collins, Kathleen, 10
comancheros, 12, 27, 99
corn farming, 66

115

Cornelia, postal station, 39
Coronado, Francisco Vásquez de, 35–36
cotton farming, 23
Cowart, P. E., 42
Curry family, 43

Dan (horse), 31–34
dancing, 46–47, 92–93
Decoration Day, 62–63
Dimmitt, Castro County, 51, 73
Dodge City, Kansas, 32
Dripping Spring (Palo Duro Canyon), 21
dugouts, 21, 55–56, 101–03, *101*
Dumas, Moore County, Texas, 26
Durham, Charley, 42
Dust Bowl, 89–91
Dye, Henry, 25, 103

elections, 11, 69, 74, 79–81
Ethel May, 80–81
Evans, Josiah, 73

Farm-to-Market Road 284, 108
farming, 23, 19–21, 64–65, 66
Farnsworth, Bob, 42
Federal Bureau of Public Roads, 11
Fisher family, 36, 64, 94
Fisher, John, 36, 94
Fisher, Willis, 71
Floyd County Historical Society, 44
Floyd County, 41–45
Floydada, Floyd County, 77
food, 19–21, 47–48, 65–68, 93, 97, 99
Formby, Marshall, 108
Fort Worth & Denver Railroad, 21, 41
Fort, Mr., 95, 96
Foster, G. G., 21
Foster, Hosea, 19–21
freighting, 41–45, *50*
Friona, Parmer County, 99, 100

games, 92–93
Gillham, Loyce, 76
Great Depression, 10, 74–75, 85–86
Green, Tom, 96
Griffith, Daff, 42

Griffith, Fred, 42
Griffith, Jim, 42
Griffith, Roy, 42
Griffith, Theo, 42

Hamblen (Scenic) Drive, map, 3; 10–11, 74–78, 103, *104*, 105–107, *106, 107*, 108–09, *110*
Hamblen, Ada Sprayberry, portraits, *57, 58*; parents; 10; child born premature, 39, 58; courted by Will, 31, 46–47, 55; marriage and family, 56–58; living in Palo Duro with Will, 101; settles with Will in Armstrong County, 82–85, 87; household chores, 89; home open for socializing, 92–93; church membership, 95
Hamblen, Alfred Beryl, 86
Hamblen, Alfred Sterling, 10, *58*, 76, 87–88
Hamblen, Claude, 51, 103
Hamblen, David "Dave," 88, 103
Hamblen, Eutha Mae Strawn, portrait, *9*; 9–10, 12; writing about Native Americans, 28
Hamblen, Fannie, 19
Hamblen, Luther Ray, 103
Hamblen, Mattie, 19
Hamblen, Nellie, *58*
Hamblen, Oleff, 86
Hamblen, Sterling Philip, 19; marriage and remarriage, 19; settles in Texas, 21–23; Indian scare, 23–24; freighting, 41; working with son in Palo Duro, 74; files on land in Palo Duro, 101–03
Hamblen, Virginia Ann Luttrell, 19, 103
Hamblen, William "Will" Henry Harrison, 11–12, 103, portraits, *4, 54, 57, 58, 110*; dream of building road, 9, 11, 17, 74, 109; runs for office, 11, 74, 79–81; parents, siblings, and birth, 19; works for living, 25–26; breaking and working with horses, 25, 31–34, 46–47, *52, 111*; premature child of, 39, 58; buys land from Mr. Bradford, 40;

courts Ada, 46–47, 55; marriage and family, 56–58, 82–86, *84*, 87; community involvement of, 69–70; working with father in Palo Duro, 74; works on road, 74–78, 81, 105–07, 108–09, *112*; builds new house, 83–85, *84*; farming and cattle trading, 55, 85, 87–88; home open for socializing, 92–93; church membership, 95; living in Palo Duro with Ada, 101; injury and death, 110
Hamblen, William Henry (grandson of Will), 86
Hamilton, Tex., 41
Hamner, Laura V., 17–18
Happy Canyon, 37; school and cemetery, 37, 38
Happy Hollow, 43
Happy Masonic Lodge 1008, 73
Happy, Swisher County, 39, 40, 43
Heisler, Charles F., 53
Heisler, Wiatt, 49, 51, 53, 88
Herndon, Judge Henry E., 11, 75
Hill, Jessie, 99
historical markers, 12, 44–45, *102,* 103, 109, *112*
Hobart, Mr. (JA Ranch manager), 53
Holt, Clay, 42
Hoover, Emma Lou Thornton, 98–99
Hoover, John Alan, 98
Hoover, Robert Alan, 98–99
horse handling, 19, 42, 48–52, 66, 74, *77,* 82–83, *83,* 99–100
Howard, Aubrey, 96
Howard, Manny, 83, 96
Hunt County, 19–21, 23

immigrant car, 21
immigrant wagon, 36
Indian trails, 10, 103, 109
Indian–settler encounters, 23–24, 97
Irick, R. M., 42, *50,* 51

JA Ranch, 23, 39, 101–02; round-up, 46–52
Jack, 80
Jake, 60–61
Jesse James gang, 100
Jo Ellen, 59–61
John, 60–61
Johnson County, Tex., 19
Johnson, Mrs. B. T., 56
Joyce, 80

Kansas City, Kansas, 73
Knight, Light, 42
Kress, Swisher County, 98
Ku Klux Klan, 19

Lakeview, Armstrong County, 103
Lane, Bessie McGehee, 40
Lane, Joyce, 40
Lane, W. I., 40
Lemmons, Mr., 39
Little Blue River, 47, 55
Lockney, Floyd County, 42–45, 77
Lott, Mr., 105, 107
Lubbock, Lubbock County, 42, 105
[Luttrell], Effie, 56–57
Luttrell, Molly, 23–24
Luttrell (Hamblen), Virginia Ann, 19, 102, 103

Mackenzie Battle Ground, 29
Mackenzie, Col. Ranald S., 12, 28–29
Madison, A. F., 39
Madison, W. F., 39
Masonry, 73
Mayo, Bole, 47
Mayo, "Grandma," 71–72
McCrerey, Mr. and Mrs. J. W., 62
McGavock, Dimple Baker, 44
McGee (Hamblen), Jane, 19
McGehee family, 94
McGehee, Clara McClain, 62, 95, 96
McGehee, Curtis, 40, 64, 72, 96
McGehee, David, 95
McGehee, Jim, 65
McGehee, John, 65, 71, 95, 107, 108–09
McGehee, "Mother," 37, 40
McGehee, Ruby, 40
McGehee, Sally, 38

McGehee, Susie (Mrs. John), 71, 95
McGehee, William David, 40
McGuffey's Reader, 21
McSpadden family, 36, 94
McSpadden, Beulah, 37–38
McSpadden, Mr., 37
medicine, 71–72
Mesquite Flat, 102, 103
Mills, Sam, 42
Moore County, 25–26
Morgan, Henry, 51
Morris, Judge Richard, 108
Mulberry, Tenn., 19
mule handling, 19, 22, 42, 66, 74, 82–83, 83
music, 92–93, 98

Native American life, 27–30
Negro Aimy, 97
Newark, Erath County, 98
Nocona, Chief [Peta], 29
Nortex Offset Publications, 10

Palo Duro Canyon State Park, 9
Palo Duro Canyon, 9, 17, 37, 61; cutting wood in, 24, 42, 59, 74, 103; Native Americans in, 27; home of Ada Sprayberry's family, 31; settlers arriving at, 35–36; fruit picking in, 65; road across, 71, 74–78, 105–07, 108–09
Pampa, Gray County, 105
Panhandle-Plains Historical Museum, 10
Park, the (Armstrong County), 37
Parker, Cynthia Ann, 12, 27, 29–30; *30*
Parker, Quanah, 12, 27–30, *30*
Parmer County, 99
[Peta] Nocona, Chief, 29
Phillips, Hutchinson County, 105
Plainview, Hale County, 41, 42, 51, 77, 108
Plemmons, Judge, 41
Posey, Walt, 42
Post-to-Borger Highway Association, 108
Prairie Dog Town Fork of the Red River, 11, 58, 77, 105, *106*, 107
Public Works Administration, 10, 75

quicksand, 32–34, 37, 77, 105
Quitaque, Briscoe County, 28, 73, 88

Ragtown (Amarillo), 41
railroads, 21, 43, 82
Ralph, 60–61
Randall County, 21
Rim to Rim, 9–10, 11–12
roads, wagon and automobile, 10–11, 71, 74–78, 105–07
Roaring Springs, Motley County, 41, 73
Rogers, Jimmy, 47
Roosevelt, President Franklin Delano, 74–75, 85
Roosevelt, President Theodore, 29–30

Salem, 94
Santa Fe Railroad, 43
Scroggins, Mr., 81
Sebastion family, 24
Silverton, Briscoe County, 11, 39, 42, 73
Six Mile crossing, 64
Slaton, Lubbock County, 43
Smith, Chili, 105, 107
Snodgrass, Harry, 42
Snodgrass, Jules, 42
sorghum farming, 19–21, 66–68
Sprayberry (Hamblen), Ada, 31,
Stewart, Charlie, 105, 107
Stinkhole Camp, 46
storms, 59, 87–88, 89–90
Strong, C. R., 73
Surginer, C., 42
Swisher County, 98, 99

Tafoya, José Piedad, 12, 27–28
Taiban, N.M., 99
Tarrant County, 97
Texas Highway 207, 9–10, 11, 17
Texas Highway Commission, 105–07
Texas Plains Trail Region, 114
thistles, 90–91
Thornton (Bussell), Sue, 98
Thornton (Hoover), Emma Lou, 98–99
Thornton, "Grandmother" Nancy Elverson, 97–100
Thornton, Jim, 42

Thornton, Napoleon "Nat" Bonaparte, 97–98, 100
Tipton family, 39
Tipton, Grandfather, 55, 57
Tipton, Grandmother, 57
Tobe Smith Flat, 107
Townsend, W. T., 73
Tule Camp, 46
Tule Canyon, 27, 28, 29
Tulia, Swisher County, 73
Turner, Mr. (Will Hamblen's employer), 25

Vigo Park, Armstrong County, 66, 95

Ward, C. T., *50,* 51
Warner, Dr., 71, 105
Wayside Baptist Church (Beulah Baptist Church), 95, 96
Wayside Community Church, 95–96, *95*
Wayside School, 10
Wayside, Armstrong County, Texas, 9, 11, 36, 39–40, 53, 64–68, 71–72, 74–75, 84, 87; community life in, 62–63, 92–93, *94,* 105, 107
Wesley, Elvin, 75–76
West Texas A&M University, 10
West Texas State College, 10
Whitman, S. C., 73
Wild Horse Lake, 41
wildfire, 59–61
Willis, Sybil Fisher, 64
Works Progress Administration, 11, 78
World War I, 82
World War II, 85–86, 107

This book was set in the Minion and
Trajan fonts using Adobe InDesign CC
on the Macintosh computer,
and digitally printed.

www.ingramcontent.com/pod-product-compliance
Lightning Source LLC
Chambersburg PA
CBHW051952290426
44110CB00015B/2210